Young People and Their Lord

Rubel Shelly

To

Michelle, Tim, and Tom

Who Walk Closely With Their Lord

And Bring Such Joy to Their Parents

Table of Contents

Introduction 1

1/ Drawing the Line 7

2/ How Honest Are You? 17

3/ Drinking Doesn't Fit 27

4/ The Drug Culture 37

5/ Pornography and Behavior 47

6/ Wholesome Sexuality 57

7/ If the Music is Off-Key 65

8/ Money Isn't Everything 75

9/ Dealing With Racial Prejudice 85

10/ Superstition, Astrology, and the Occult 97

11/ A Bridle For Your Tongue 111

12/ Blushing Is a Healthy Sign 119

13/ Power to Do Right 129

Introduction

This book is not written to explain how one becomes a Christian. It is written to help young men and women who are already Christians understand the *practical meaning of living for Christ* in an evil age.

Salvation is by grace through faith in Jesus (Rom. 3:21-26; Eph. 2:8-9). We are not saved because we are moral, decent, and upright persons. No one can be good enough to earn God's fellowship, for "all have sinned and fall short of the glory of God" (Rom. 3:23). We are saved because Christ offered himself to take the death-blow we were due to suffer. He went to the cross, taking our sin upon himself. "But he was pierced for our transgressions, he was crushed for our iniquities; the punishment that brought us peace was upon him, and by his wounds we are healed" (Isa. 53:5).

The *gospel* is the good news that God has provided redemption to unworthy people through his infinite mercy. Rule-keeping is not the basis of our hope (Rom. 3:20). Our hope rests on Christ and the right-standing God gives us through him. As we say it in song: "My hope is built on nothing less than Jesus' blood and righteousness."

Having said this, however, some want to stop the redemption story. They do not emphasize that *saved people in Christ are called to live a changed life.* Here is what Paul said: "Everyone who confesses the name of the Lord must turn away from wickedness" (2 Tim. 2:19b). The Christian message is left incomplete if we fail to teach its implications for a radical change in daily life.

1

There are distinct moral consequences to the teachings of Christ and the apostles. This book attempts to make some of those consequences clear to young believers.

To say it another way, think of Pentecost for a moment. When Christ was preached on that day, men and women who sought salvation from their sins were told: "Repent and be baptized, every one of you, in the name of Jesus Christ so that your sins may be forgiven. And you will receive the gift of the Holy Spirit"(Acts 2:38).Christ has earned (1) forgiveness and (2) power to overcome for those who believe in him.

Most of us understand the part about having sins forgiven; fewer of us seem to be aware of the "gift of the Holy Spirit" and its meaning for our lives. Most Christians know they are supposed to overcome and put to death the sinful things of their past. "Put to death, therefore, whatever belongs to your earthly nature: sexual immorality, impurity, lust, evil desires and greed, which is idolatry. ... But now you must rid yourselves of all such things as these: anger, rage, malice, slander, filthy language" (Col. 3:5,8). But how?

No one can conquer sin through his or her own strength. Sin can be defeated only in the strength God provides Christians through the indwelling Spirit. "If *by the Spirit you put to death the misdeeds of the body,* you will live" (Rom. 8:13b). Both forgiveness of past sins and power to live in newness of life are divine gifts. Some of us want to claim the former without the latter. They are designed to go together. [Note: The work of the Holy Spirit in helping young Christians live godly and happy lives will be studied in Chapter Thirteen.]

Christians in the first century were known because of their different way of life. Their commitment to purity in an impure environment was a powerful statement to their contemporaries. It caused many to take the case for Christianity seriously who were caught up in — but miserable because of — a lifestyle of license, drunkenness, sexual sin, and materialism. They saw divine power at work in the transformation of people who had once lived as they were living. They wanted to know how it could happen in their lives.

Your commitment to honesty, truthfulness, chastity, and the other virtues which belong to Christianity will be your most powerful statement to people who know you. It will become the opening for you to lead people who do not know the Savior to hear the gospel message and be saved!

A Ford dealer who drives Chevrolets probably won't be successful in selling his product. People will wonder why he drives a car other than the ones he is trying to sell. Christians who live no differently from their non-Christian friends won't be successful in sharing Christ.

We need to understand and accept the demands of discipleship. And that is what this book is about. It focuses on the theme of *living under the Lordship of Christ.* A conversion to Christ which does not reach the level of daily behavior is fundamentally flawed. The goal of this book is to help young Christians carry through on your commitment to the Lord Jesus.

Special thanks must be given to the Family of God at Ashwood and to 20th Century Christian for making it possible for me to devote my time to a writing ministry. A gracious God has been willing to place my life in close association with the good people of a great church and a respected publishing firm in order to give me the chance to do what I enjoy most. With the joy of such an association comes a tremendous sense of responsibility.

Amy Jones worked above and beyond the call of duty to assist me in getting the original edition of *Young People and Their Lord* completed within self-imposed time limits which were very rigid. Similarly, Teresa Stephens was the key person in producing this revision of the book.

Finally, I thank my wife, Myra, and our three children (to whom this book is dedicated) for their help. At the time this book went to press in its original form, Michelle was 19, Tim was 16, and Tom was 13 — *three teen-agers in the same house at the same time.* At the time of this edition, three years have passed, and a host of events has come and gone — including a wedding and the beginning of college for the older two. Other than my own memories of personal teen-age years, their shared experiences tell me most about the things young people need in order to live under the Lordship of Jesus. They are handling their teen experience with so much more maturity than I ever did! I thank God for their Christian commitment and beautiful spirits. They even read the text of this book and helped me with the final writing of it.

May God bless you in reading, thinking, doing, and *growing* in the Lord.

Rubel Shelly
Nashville, TN

1 / Drawing the Line

Karen said she had felt alone and unloved. Her parents "didn't understand" her feelings — and didn't seem to take her seriously. Then she met Rick. He was warm, sympathetic, and really cared about her. They began having sex on their third date. Now she was pregnant, and Rick was dating someone else. She told me she wanted to die and was planning her suicide. I felt that my conversation with her might either push her over the edge or give her hope to hang on.

He had been sent home from school because he was drunk. His parents were upset and didn't know what to do about it. They were just sure that their son had accidentally "fallen in with the wrong crowd." So they asked me to talk with Jerry. Jerry's story was different, though. This was nothing new to him, for he had been drinking heavily for a year — though he was only a junior in high school. He didn't drink with his school friends or at their suggestion. He drank alone. Occasionally he smoked marijuana. "No," he said, "I don't know why I started. I just know I can't stop now."

Cases like those of Karen and Jerry could be multiplied many times over. Bright, good-looking, talented — but unhappy, insecure, and bored with life. Thus they get caught up with sex, drugs, shoplifting, or one of a dozen other risk-taking involvements which destroy many of them.

Among 15-to-24-year-olds across America, suicide is the third leading cause of death. Only homicide and accidents take more young lives in this country than suicide. In my home state of Tennessee, it is the second leading cause of death among adolescents. A report released in the spring of 1987 by the Tennessee Department of Mental Health placed suicide behind accidents and ahead of homicide in the state.

Since 1950 the number of teen suicides has tripled among people 15 to 24 to around 6,000 annually. Researchers at the National Institute of Mental Health report that attempted suicides outnumber actual suicides somewhere between 10 and 100 to one. Some physicians are especially alarmed about a rise in cases of anorexia nervosa, a syndrome in which young people (mostly females) starve themselves into virtual skeletons; they think anorexia may be a thinly disguised form of suicide. Still other experts in the field believe that some of the deaths of teens which are classified as accidental by law enforcement agencies are actually suicide cases.

Why so much disenchantment? The threat of nuclear war, overprotection by parents, media-induced passivity, broken homes — all these and many more explanations have been offered. While one must be careful not to give a quick and shallow answer to such a complex question, there does seem to be a common thread among the most troubled of today's teens.

Mary Giffin, author of *A Cry for Help,* writes: "Over and over, the [suicidal] adolescents...groped for words to describe what they felt was a void in their lives — the lack of anything to stand for, of an altruistic goal."

It makes sense. Anyone with a *why* for living will find a *how.* If you have a *goal,* you have hope; if you have *hope,* you won't destroy yourself with a gun, drugs, rebellion, or boredom.

The time has come to *draw the line* against hopelessness and depression. There is a way to live with joy and purpose. Jesus Christ is the central factor in a truly meaningful life, and living under his Lordship is the response of a Christian which makes life full and rewarding.

There Are Some Problems

The sad truth of the matter is that the same wave of hopeless despair which has washed over many non-Christian young people has overwhelmed some Christian teens. Young people are dropping out of the church and giving up on Christianity. Compare the number of children in third-grade Sunday school class with the number of teens in the high school class. In a church which has 20 in the third-grade class, most would feel good about a combined high school class which totals 15.

The two incidents related at the beginning of this chapter involved teens who are church members. Just having your name on the church roll is not going to guarantee a meaningful life.

I can't give numbers on the percentage of Christian teens who are struggling unsuccessfully with life. A look at some broader studies among young people in the United States might be helpful to stimulate reflection.

Gallup polls report that 40 percent of all teens believe in astrology, 93 percent know their sign, and 30 percent read astrology columns regularly. Six of ten believe high school students should have access to contraceptives — and almost exactly the same percentage (58 percent) of teen-age members of Protestant churches agree. Gallup says that 65 percent of teens who are members of evangelical churches never read their Bibles, ånd 33 percent believe religion is out-of-date and out-of-touch with their lives.

A major study done by Catholic University in Washington, D.C., showed that 32 percent of Catholic youth, 34 percent of Baptists, and 25 percent of Methodist youth profess a need for religion in their lives but "cannot relate to the present church."

What is going on? Can you honestly say things are significantly better in your own home church? The gospel of Christ seems to have made little difference in the lives of many young people.

The Bible Gives Counsel

The Bible speaks to young people with inspired counsel about living. Some of the counsel is negative in nature and warns against things which will harm and destroy; some is positive and shows the alternative which believers adopt in preference to Satan's enticements.

"How can a young man keep his way pure? By living according to your word. I will seek you with all my heart; do not let me stray from your commands. I have hidden your word in my heart that I might not sin against you. Praise be to you, O Lord; teach me your decrees" (Psa. 119:9-12).

Much of the teaching of young people in the church has been built around a mistaken interpretation of this verse which declares: Give young people the facts from the Bible and they will live spiritual lives. Wrong! This verse assumes something which we have been prone to overlook. It is written against the background of a *personal relationship* with God. Because David knew and loved God, he could take the next step of learning and following his commandments. Try to teach the commandments without that relationship, and the result is neutral at best and likely negative in nature.

The Bible is not an end in itself. It points to a *person* and seeks to bring men and women into a relationship with him. Until that relationship is established, all the knowledge in the world will be insufficient to change a life.

If one knows and loves Jesus Christ, she will submit her heart and life to the absolutes of the Word of God; the application of those truths to her life will change her life experience and result in transformation. The good result she sees and demonstrates in her life becomes more proof to her that her life is on the right course (cf. Rom. 12:1-2).

On the other hand, one who does not have such a relationship with Jesus can evaluate what is offered him only from the narrow perspective of his personal life experience. If he sees no reward to himself from the demand being made or possibly even a sacrifice being required, he will turn away.

If the difference between these two models is still fuzzy in your mind, take a concrete example of how it works. Take the biblical injunction against fornication as a case in point. The one who knows Jesus decides what her attitude toward sex prior to marriage will be on the basis of the Word of God. Since she believes that Jesus is the Son of God, her devotion to him causes her to accept his command about chastity. Faced with peer pressure or improper desires within her own heart, she has a fixed point of reference for decision-making. On the other hand, perhaps the boy she is dating is not a Christian. Because he does not know Jesus, he cannot see things as she does or understand her attitude. He decides what he believes and does on the basis of what makes him feel good or gives him status within a certain group. Because the girl is attractive, sex is exciting, and his friends and he can see nothing wrong with sex before marriage, he wants to take her to bed.

Even some young people who are church members have the attitude of the young man described above. Because Jesus is only a name and Christianity nothing more than a do-and-don't chart, they cannot maintain a lifestyle that is truly Christian.

How Jesus Makes a Difference

The gospel message offers an alternative that is sound and practical. The Lord Jesus Christ can bring meaning, hope, and purpose into a frustrated life.

Because young people are **relationship oriented,** you need to see Jesus Christ in his personal dimensions as your Savior. *Christianity is not principally concerned with smoking, drinking, astrology, and the like (cf. Rom. 14:17). It is about the Eternal Word loving you so much that he gave up certain of his divine rights to come to earth, take your sins upon himself, and die for you (John 1:1-14; Phil. 2:5-11).* He did not come to bring you a list of rules but to lay down his life for you. Because of who he is and what he has done, you will want to learn and live by the principles which will help you conform to his example. But start with the person of Jesus and the significance of his life for yours. Everything about Jesus centers on his cross — the death, burial, and resurrection. It was there that he took your sins upon himself and offers you right-standing with heaven. "God made him who had no sin to be sin for us, so that in him we might become the righteousness of God" (2 Cor. 5:21). When you allow him to save you, you commit your life to him. You begin to "live a new life" (Rom. 6:1-4).

Because young people **long for acceptance,** you will be thrilled to realize that Jesus has accepted you. Sin and guilt are the same in the lives of teen-agers as they are in older people. Sin hurts, and guilt consumes. The experience of sin and guilt makes you know how unworthy you are before a holy God. Thus you tend to pull back from him and from the church.

But forgiven people are accepted people. Once you are in Christ, your sins have been forgiven by the cleansing power of the blood of Jesus. They will never be held against you again. When you sin again in your new life as a Christian, divine grace prohibits the sin from being held against you. So long as you remain humble, sorry about your sins, and teachable, the blood of Jesus continues to cleanse you and keep you free of condemnation (1 John 1:7; cf. Rom. 4:8; 8:1). Accepted by Christ, the church serves as his arms to hold and support you when you are struggling with sin.

Because young people need **a cause to serve,** Christ places you in his spiritual body and allows you to serve him there. The same process that saves you automatically places you in the church (Acts 2:47). Not only does that church hold and support you within its fellowship, but it also gives you an outlet for doing good and bringing glory to the one who has saved you (Eph. 2:10).

For a Christian to confess "Jesus is *Lord*" is to say that he or she recognizes Jesus as the Divine Sovereign who reigns over his or her life. This takes us back to the matter of living under absolutes, which was mentioned earlier in this chapter. It introduces the concept of **discipleship.** It also opens the possibility of being one through whom Jesus reaches to others — **evangelism.** If Jesus Christ is a living and reigning reality in your life, others will see and desire what you have. You can point them to the one who has saved you as the one who can give meaning and purpose to their lives.

Because young people need **a moral code to live by,** daily growth in the Word of God will allow you to build an increasing stability into your life. A lack of clear moral standards in one's life leads to confusion, confusion leads to sinful involvement with things of this world, and sin destroys the beauty of life — only to replace it with the odor of death.

You are at an early point in life where moral decisions are complicated by a lack of personal experience. Since you have not lived long enough to know the nature of certain deeds or the consequences that come with them, you need some trusted source for moral guidance. The Word of God is available to you for that purpose.

Although you may feel confused at times, there is no reason to despair or give up. You can have a relationship with Christ as your Savior and Lord, know that you have been forgiven and accepted in Jesus, discover a cause to serve in his church, and live by a practical moral code which has been made known in Scripture.

Guidelines About Right and Wrong

Since this book focuses particular attention on the matter of right living as God's child, it will be necessary for us to agree on the method to be used in the remainder of this volume. How can you help yourself and others to determine right and wrong?

Since we acknowledge Jesus Christ and the absolutes he has revealed in his example and words, the following four guidelines will be appealed to time after time in dealing with the issues to be treated later in this book:

1. Does the Bible explicitly approve or condemn the matter in question?

This is to ask whether there is a "You shall ..." or "You shall not ..." statement about the action. For example, obeying parents is commanded and lying is forbidden; these are actions covered by explicit statements.

2. Is there a biblical principle which is directly related to the matter?

The Bible could not possibly list every approved or disapproved action in human behavior. It would be an incredibly large volume which no one could master. But it does identify basic principles of human behavior (e.g., the Golden Rule, Matt. 7:12) which are to guide our decision-making as followers of Christ. For example, gambling is not discussed in terms of an explicit prohibition, but certain fundamental principles of biblical morality allow us to determine that it is wrong.

3. What effect will it have on my influence as a child of God?

People who are serious about living under the Lordship of Jesus take this guideline to heart. We desire to imitate Christ and to bring others to him. Thus we must not become involved in things which would compromise our allegiance to Christ in the eyes of unbelievers. If an action consistently puts one in evil company, causes him to be absent from assemblies of the church, or leads others to question his commitment to the Lord, he should forego any involvement in it.

4. What is the advice of the best people I know about the matter in question?

This test is less objective than the previous three. Yet it is important for Christians who are young in years and faith to realize that more mature children of God have had valuable experience in living under Lordship which enables them to use good judgment about human behavior. A parent, elder, or preacher might be able to give counsel about certain matters which would be extremely helpful. While such persons are not infallible, one should be slow to set aside their advice.

Conclusion

Here is an important text to fix in your mind as we begin: "For the grace of God that brings salvation has appeared to all men. It teaches us to say 'No' to ungodliness and worldly passions, and to live self-controlled, upright and

14

godly lives in this present age, while we wait for the blessed hope — the glorious appearing of our great God and Savior, Jesus Christ, who gave himself for us to redeem us from all wickedness and to purify for himself a people that are his very own, eager to do what is good" (Tit. 2:11-14).

Remember that your salvation is based on the grace of God — not your good character or good works. At the same time, remember that grace is not cheap. It demands that believers — young and old — learn to say an emphatic "No" to sin. Redeemed from its guilt and power, we dare not continue to flirt with or dabble in sin. To the contrary, we must live self-controlled, upright, and godly lives. And we must say an emphatic "Yes" to all that is good and which glorifies our God.

Then we will be able to look forward to the return of Jesus Christ. The personal Savior who has redeemed us and seen us through life's struggles will return to claim us.

A youth minister who was concerned about the spiritual coldness of the teens he worked with prayed for and sought a means to impress them with their need for a truly Christian lifestyle. He came up with the idea of challenging his youth group to reach out to a group of severely handicapped children.

The teens spent a day taking the children to a rodeo. It took nearly half an hour just to load and unload the handicapped kids from their wheelchairs onto the bus. All day they took care of the children by pushing, feeding, and cleaning up after them. Finally, they took the children home, unloaded them, and reboarded the bus.

Standing before the church group, the leader said, "I'm very proud of all of you, but I have some questions. How many of you are grieved that some of those kids don't even know where they have been today?" Several raised their hands.

"How many of you hurt that these kids won't even remember you or what you did for them?" More hands went up.

Then he said, "What hurts me is that most of you are as handicapped to God as those kids are to you."

With that he sat down and drove the silent bus back to

the parking lot of the church building. A noticeable difference began to be made in the lives of many of the group
from that day forward. They had lived a principle which is
sometimes hard to grasp.

What about you? Don't turn back from following the one
who has saved you. Don't be content to be spiritually handicapped and retarded in your relationship with a loving
Redeemer who has saved you by his grace.

2 / How Honest Are You?

Madison Sarratt taught mathematics for several years at Vanderbilt University. Before each exam he administered, he would say, "Today I am giving two examinations — one in trigonometry and the other in honesty. I hope you will pass them both. If you must fail one, fail trigonometry. There are many good people in the world who can't pass trigonometry, but there are no good people who cannot pass the examination of honesty."

William Taylor, owner of a medical-supply firm in San Diego, picked up $2,400 in cash which was blowing down the street. He took it to the police. The person to whom the money belonged was found. He had withdrawn the money from his bank, laid it in an envelope on top of his car, and driven off. Someone asked Mr. Taylor why he would want to turn in the money rather than just keep it and say nothing. "I felt it was my duty," he said. "From giving the money back, I've had the personal satisfaction of actually doing what my conscience told me was the right thing to do." After the incident was reported in the newspapers, his company received about 50 calls from people praising him for his deed — and offering to send their business to his company.

Christian character has many different elements. One which needs a great deal of emphasis in our day is personal integrity and honesty. "Therefore, each of you must put off

17

falsehood and speak truthfully to his neighbor, for we are all members of one body" (Eph. 4:25).

A. Ernest Fitzgerald was fired from his job as an Air Force financial analyst in 1969 after he exposed a two-billion-dollar overrun on a contract. He was restored to his old job in 1982 when it was established in court that his dismissal was directly related to political pressures designed to intimidate him — and other "whistle blowers." Senator William Proxmire says of him: "He is a rare gem — extremely bright and a man of absolute integrity." Back on the job again, he has testified recently about Pentagon purchases of $7 claw hammers for $436 and $0.25 washers for $693.

Does learning about an episode such as Mr. Fitzgerald's make you angry? What about graft among political officials, cheating by welfare recipients, insider trading on the stock market, or the practice of contractors who use shoddy building materials and charge premium prices to buyers? Tax evasion, shoplifting, the use of steroids by athletes, point-shaving in sports events — the list goes on and on.

Before you get too burned up about cheating and dishonesty in these public contexts, reflect for a moment on one of the most sensitive areas of ethical concern among young people: **classroom cheating.**

Is classroom cheating widespread where you are? Is it generally accepted among your friends? From studies conducted by several researchers in different parts of the country, it appears that cheating in the classroom is a widespread and growing phenomenon. These same studies also indicate that it is not usually the D or F student who cheats to avoid failing; it is the better student who is shooting for an A or B who is more likely to resort to dishonesty.

Made suspicious by her behavior during a previous exam, I watched a freshman college student in my class closely and saw her copy off another student's paper, pull some loose notes out of a notebook, and even open her textbook. Confronted with it, she began lying and denied everything. She finally realized it was hopeless and admitted what had happened. Her exact words were: "This is how I got through high school." She never showed any sign of remorse about what she had done.

Morality in the classroom is an important consideration for a young Christian. Since the major responsibility of a teen-ager in our society is the securing of an education, this is a primary setting for young Christians to prove the genuineness of their commitment to Jesus as Lord.

Seeing the Problem

A dictionary definition of the verb *cheat* is "to deceive by trickery, defraud, swindle"; the word implies dishonesty or deception which is designed to obtain an unfair advantage for oneself.

With this definition in mind, it is not difficult to realize that cheating involves more than looking over someone's shoulder during a test. Turning in homework that has been copied, reporting outside reading you did not actually do, submitting a term paper someone else wrote, and changing answers on papers graded in class are all forms of classroom cheating. One should also realize that *giving* answers to someone on an exam or doing a report for a friend is equally as deceptive and dishonest as *receiving* such work. Some people even have small-scale businesses going in high schools and colleges to sell reports, term papers, or old exams.

A poll of 2,000 students at Johns Hopkins University brought an admission that 30 percent of them had cheated at some point during their college careers. A similar poll at Stanford University showed 45 percent of the students surveyed admitting at least one serious cheating offense during their time at that school.

A 16-question form dealing with classroom ethics was developed at the University of California at Long Beach and has been used at several schools in the early- to mid-1980s. UCLB students responding to the questionnaire showed 60 percent admitting to some form of cheating. At Memphis State University, 56 percent of a group of 327 who used the same questionnaire said they occasionally cheated in school; 88 percent said they would not turn in a fellow student if they saw him or her cheating.

Even more frightening is the fact that a questionnaire on cheating which was circulated recently among 300 students at a Christian college shows 34 percent of them admitting to cheating on exams and homework during their high school years.

All these facts and figures have the effect of saying that there is a certain "difficulty" in being honest at school. Cheating is so common among students — whether in junior high, high school, or college — that it is harder to be uninvolved in it than to participate! This "difficulty" is compounded by the attitude of some teachers and school officials. They seem to ignore what they know is going on and sometimes refuse to deal with cases of cheating that are called to their attention. This makes some students wonder why they should bother to be honest.

Then what of the good student who refuses to *get* information by cheating but is pressured by classmates to *give* it? This sort of pressure is not easy to resist, for no one wants to turn people against himself or be accused of self-righteousness.

Determining to be honest in your work at school — as well as in the rest of your life — will not always be easy. Some of your classmates will not appreciate your honesty. They may ask to see your answers on an exam and get mad if you refuse. Still others will try to involve you in their cheating by offering to let you see stolen test questions before an examination or by encouraging you to turn in false reading reports along with them.

A Christian Perspective

The Bible frequently and consistently condemns dishonesty, lying, or any other form of cheating.

For example, Solomon listed seven things which are "detestable" to God, and no less than three of the seven relate to dishonesty — a lying tongue, a heart that devises wicked schemes, and a false witness who pours out lies (Prov. 6:16-19). It is no wonder that heaven hates all such conduct among human beings, for deception and trickery are devices of the devil. Satan is a subtle swindler (cf. Gen. 3:1) and "a liar and the father of lies" (John 8:44). Dishonesty is a characteristic of the Prince of Evil, and Christians are committed to follow the Prince of Righteousness.

One who knows the Bible well remembers such shameful incidents as Abraham's half-truth (Gen. 20:2, 5, 12; cf. 12:10-20), the outright dishonesty of Ananias and Sapphira (Acts 5:1-11), and James' harsh rebuke of rich men who had cheated workmen of their wages (Jas. 5:14). You probably remember, too, that "all liars" will be banished from the presence of God in eternity (Rev. 21:8).

It appears that people of every generation have been eager to believe the dictum of Pragmatism — "Whatever *works* is right." Thus they have been quick to say or do whatever seems to serve their selfish best interests at the moment. It is that very same short-sighted view of life that leads a person to think that falsifying a homework assignment, turning in a term paper he did not write, or copying answers on an exam is the thing to do.

Athletic competition was once encouraged as a character-building experience which taught fair play. Winning, however, seems to be all that matters now. Sure, winning is important. But win by talent and ability rather than unfair tactics. If you lose, be self-controlled and gracious; no one is at his or her best all the time. Being a brat on a tennis court, a "dirty player" on the basketball team, or a quick-tempered and brawling fan is a poor advertisement for your personal character and your Savior.

A Christian has a different perspective on life. He has been saved by Jesus Christ, who is "the Truth" personified (John 14:6) and can follow him only by living in truth and integrity. Just as Paul "renounced secret and shameful ways" in preaching the gospel (2 Cor. 4:2), a Christian renounces deception and unfair tactics in her life as a student or athlete.

Honesty, self-control, and truthfulness are not just the *best* policy for Christians — but *the only policy.*

21

Three Suggestions About Honesty

It will require effort for a young Christian to maintain his or her integrity. How can it be done? Here are three suggestions which will help.

First, fix a **conscious determination in your heart** to be honest in all things.

Since a person's conduct is governed by the thoughts and purposes of the heart (cf. Prov. 4:23), a teen-ager who wishes to follow Christ must look ahead to anticipate temptations he knows will come his way and then settle in his heart what his reaction will be. He must make up his mind in advance, rather than in the pressure-packed moment of temptation, about what he will do when others around him are cheating, breaking rules, or taking unfair advantage.

Daniel is a good example of a man who set his heart to do right and whose firm determination helped him avoid sinning against the Lord. When he was exiled to Babylon following a raid on Jerusalem in 606 B.C., Daniel was one of several young men judged capable of receiving special training for positions of trust within the government. It was decided that he would be taught the "language and literature of the Babylonians" and be given a "daily amount of food and wine from the king's table" (Dan. 1:4-5).

Since Daniel was a devout Jew who knew the dietary regulations of the Law of Moses, this put him in a dilemma. Many of the foods served from the king's table were "unclean" to Jewish people. Should Daniel compromise his convictions and offend God by eating those foods? Should he refuse the foods and run the risk of offending the king and losing his favored position? Here is the decision he made: "But Daniel resolved not to defile himself with the royal food and wine, and he asked the chief official for permission not to defile himself this way" (Dan. 1:8).

When one has formed a deep commitment to refuse something he knows to be wrong, he has taken a major step toward defeating that evil. Daniel thought about the problem in advance. This meant that he would not be taken by surprise or tempted with his guard down. Then, by having a purpose already formed on how he would react, he was not left to make his decision in the heat of temptation. A wise young person will learn from this example.

If you wait until the temptation is actually on you to decide how to handle it, you will be at a tremendous disadvantage. It is hard to think straight when Satan is throwing a severe temptation in your face. So think about it in advance, make a clear decision about how it ought to be handled, and then follow through on your determination.

Meeting the temptation to be dishonest in academics, athletics, or with money in a firm and determined manner instead of with halting uncertainty can make the difference.

Second, remember that **dishonesty will reflect unfavorably on Christ and your influence for him.**

It is no secret that non-Christians watch the lives of people who say we are followers of Jesus with a jaundiced and critical eye. They are eager to see something wrong in our behavior, for they are looking for an excuse to villify the Christian faith (cf. 1 Tim. 5:14; 6:1).

Your influence over friends and classmates will be forfeited if you participate in classroom dishonesty. If you have already been involved in wrong behavior, you will have to change before you can represent Christ before them. After all, it is not in the church building or Sunday school class that you are tested; the real test of your allegiance to Christ comes at school, at work, at home, and at play. What do you do when temptation comes to be dishonest? That situation becomes your opportunity to prove your commitment to Jesus as Lord by handling the situation to his glory.

Third, **be honest in spite of the possible consequences.**

It has already been pointed out that tremendous pressures can be put on a young person to participate in classroom cheating or other forms of dishonesty. It takes a great deal of courage to remain uninvolved. One risks losing "friends" (?) and making enemies.

The Savior never promised his followers that it would be easy to walk in his steps. Doing the *right* thing sometimes involves doing an *unpopular* thing. But there is something worse than suffering for doing right. There is the terrible suffering that comes from a guilty conscience now and the eternal consequences of sin which will be faced in the world to come.

When one must do wrong to escape some unpleasantness, it is the will of God that he or she suffer rather than sin. "Blessed are those who are persecuted because of righteousness, for theirs is the kingdom of heaven. Blessed are you when people insult you, persecute you and falsely say all kinds of evil against you because of me" (Matt. 5:10-11). "Be faithful, even to the point of death, and I will give you the crown of life" (Rev. 2:10).

Conclusion

Going back to Chapter One, let's apply the four "Guidelines About Right and Wrong" to the matter of integrity in the classroom. Although there is no explicit statement in the Word of God about a young person's honesty on reports, exams, and the athletic field, there are certainly biblical principles which apply very directly. Every verse in the Bible about truthfulness, honesty, and the like points to your spiritual obligation before God; every verse about lying, deception, and trickery warns against cheating or taking unfair advantage. The matter of your Christian influence has already been discussed at some length. And you certainly wouldn't expect any mature Christian you know to recommend dishonesty to you. By the guidelines we agreed on at the beginning of this book, the conclusion we must reach about cheating seems pretty obvious.

Paul Ginsburg, dean of students on one of the campuses of the University of Wisconsin, asked this pessimistic question about cheating in school classrooms: "What can you do about it when it is a reflection of the rest of society?"

The young person who lives under Jesus' Lordship has a reply to make to that fatalistic inquiry. He or she can say: "I have made a commitment to Jesus Christ, and part of that commitment involves my pledge not to let the world set my standards. Even if everyone else — in school and in the rest of society — insists that cheating and other forms of dishonesty are acceptable actions, my duty remains clear. My life is supposed to reflect Christ to the world, not the other way around!"

3 / Drinking Doesn't Fit

Bubba Smith appeared in the highly successful Lite Beer commercials for several years. He quit in 1986. In an Associated Press account of his decision, he is quoted as saying, "I didn't know what it was doing to the kids. Once I saw it, I thought, I'm not going to do it any more. How much money can you make before you ruin everybody?" He said he made his decision after serving as grand marshall in the Michigan State University homecoming parade. "I thought everyone was very fired up. All of a sudden one side of the street started saying, 'Tastes great,' and the other side would answer, 'Less filling.' It just totally freaked me out. When I went to the bonfire, they were just completely drunk out of their heads. It was a thing that came down that I was selling to children, because children watch football a lot, and that's when a lot of the time slots are bought." Bubba isn't selling any more beer after that experience.

There was no officially sanctioned drinking at the senior prom, but a few of the guys had taken some six-packs of beer in their cars. Some were passed around. The really heavy drinking began after the dance was over. It lasted into the early morning hours. There were seven people in the car, and all were intoxicated. Nobody even knows for sure who was driving. The automobile was making between 80 and 100 mph when it slammed into the side of a tractor-trailer at an intersection. Four young men and three young women were not alive to graduate with their classmates.

Imagine that we discover a powerful drug that occurs rather freely and spontaneously in nature. Used sparingly and with good judgment, that drug can be used for a refreshing tension reliever.

Suppose, however, that instead of using the drug sparingly and with good judgment, it begins to be generally misused. Suppose further that research over a period of years reveals that it is addicting to a consistent percentage of all who use it, is implicated in several serious diseases, and has damaging side-effects on those who use it regularly over long periods of time. Suppose also that it becomes a social problem responsible for billions of dollars in property damage, half of all deaths on the highways, half of all murders in the country, and a third of all suicides.

What would be the proper response for a Christian to make toward that drug and its general availability? Would there be justification for Christian teen-agers mounting a campaign against its use by their peers or even for its banishment from society? Surely none of us would defend its easy availability, keep it in our homes, or distribute it among our friends.

You're way ahead of me by now, aren't you? This imaginary scenario has its real-life equivalent in the history of *alcohol abuse*. This chapter will explore something of the attitude young Christians should take toward alcohol in this culture.

Is Alcohol Use Sinful?

The analogy used above concerning the imaginary drug seems to be a good one for alcohol. It appears unreasonble to argue that there is anything intrinsically evil about alcohol or beverages containing alcohol. If it were used in a context where no harm followed, why would anyone feel compelled to oppose its use?

But that isn't the history of alcohol. Alcohol — in spite of the good properties it possesses — has not been used innocently. Once discovered and known, it has come to be spotlighted in society not for its positive values but for its negative ones.

Alcohol addicts a consistent percentage of all the people who use it. There are 12 to 15 million alcoholics in this country; approximately one-fourth are teen-agers. National studies show that as many as 30 percent of all high-school students in the United States are problem drinkers. The same studies reveal that around 56 percent of teens nationwide take their first drink in the ninth grade or earlier. And early drinkers are the ones most likely to grow up into adult alcoholics.

Alcohol consumption is implicated in several diseases. A report published by the United States Department of Health, Education, and Welfare says: "Alcohol is indisputably involved in the causation of cancer and its consumption is one of the few types of exposure known to increase the risk of cancer at various sites in the human body." The body sites named in the report were the mouth and pharynx, larynx, esophagus, liver, and lung. As an editorial in the *Journal of the American Medical Association* pointed out recently, "Most physicians are aware that alcohol is a direct toxin and that alcohol abuse can adversely affect every body system."

A Congressional report released in 1983 claims that alcohol abuse costs the economy of the United States as much as $120 billion a year. Dr. Leonard Saxe, principal author of the report, said the average alcoholic cost society about $10,000 in 1982. Medicare paid doctors and hospitals $150 million for the treatment of alcoholism in the same year.

Drinking drivers are more of a threat to American lives than war. More than 250,000 persons have been killed in the last ten years in auto accidents involving alcohol. By comparison, there were 53,513 American battle deaths in World War I, 292,131 in World War II, 33,629 in the Korean War, and 47,752 in the Vietnam War. Fifty percent of all auto fatalities are directly traceable to someone who has been drinking.

The horrible statistics go on and on. Alcohol is involved in 80 percent of all home violence, 50 percent of all murders, 30 percent of all suicides, 60 percent of all child abuse, and 65 percent of all drownings. According to a report released by the Bureau of Justice Statistics in 1985, 54 percent of jail inmates convicted of violent crimes had been drinking just before committing the crimes for which they were serving time. Almost seven of every 10 people convicted of manslaughter had been drinking before their crime; 62 percent of those convicted of assault had been drinking; 49 percent of those convicted of murder or attempted murder had been drinking. Do you think the involvement of alcohol was coincidental in these cases? Very heavy drinking was most prevalent among criminals between the ages of 18 and 25.

If we had hard data concerning any other drug which even approached these for alcohol, that drug would not be available as an over-the-counter item in supermarkets! Yet it is available to everyone in this society, and young people can get their hands on it without difficulty. Even with the raised drinking age across the country, there is always a "friend" who can secure it for you.

Some things are intrinsically evil (i.e., evil in and of themselves). Examples of such sins would be blasphemy, lying, and murder. They contradict the inherent holiness of God and dishonor his image in man.

Other things, though not intrinsically evil, can become evil by virtue of their effects. In light of 1 Corinthians 6:12-13, the two primary tests of such things would be as follows: (1) Are they generally harmful to those who participate in their use? (2) Do they enslave their users? Alcohol certainly seems to be a prime candidate for inclusion under this heading.

Some Biblical Data

Did Noah discover alcoholic beverage? That's doubtful! Noah does have the dubious distinction of being the first fellow we meet in Scripture who gets into trouble because of its use (cf. Gen. 9:20-23). Up until that time, Noah may have used it without harm; he may have served it to his family. But on a given day, Noah used it to the point that he became intoxicated. Under the influence of alcohol, he did something he would not have done normally. With his inhibitions taken away by alcohol, he offended God and somehow implicated one of his own sons in the deed.

We just don't know who discovered alcohol, nor do we know how long it may have been used before it became such a troublemaker. What a shame that it could not have been used properly, for its constructive properties. But because it has been used the way it has, there is a consistent attitude toward alcohol that surfaces throughout Scripture.

"Woe to that wreath, the pride of Ephraim's drunkards, to the fading flower, his glorious beauty, set on the head of a fertile valley — to that city, the pride of those laid low by wine! ... And these also stagger from wine and reel from beer: Priests and prophets stagger from beer and are befuddled with wine; they reel from beer, they stagger when seeing visions, they stumble when rendering decisions. All the tables are covered with vomit and there is not a spot without filth" (Isa. 28:1, 7-8). "Old wine and new ... take away the understanding of my people" (Hos. 4:11-12a). "Wine is a mocker and beer a brawler; whoever is led astray by them is not wise" (Prov. 20:1; cf. 23:29-32).

Because of similar harm to humanity observed in various societies and cultures due to alcohol, religious people have generally stood together in days gone by to cry against its use. Proposals to legalize liquor by the drink once united any city's religious community in protest. It is no longer so. Today there are many who plead not for the banning of alcohol among Christians but for moderate and responsible use of it. Is that a reasonable position for you to take?

A Responsible Position

In all candor, I don't know of any statement in Scripture that gives the explicit command that one must totally abstain from alcoholic beverages. The use and abuse of alcohol may vary in different cultures, and thus it could be reevaluated as to the rightness or wrongness of it in terms of those cultures and its history therein. After all, alcohol is not *intrinsically* evil.

But in *our* culture, at *this* point in history, and given the principles to which God has called his people, I can defend only one attitude toward the use of beverage alcohol. I appeal

31

for anyone who wishes to honor God and live under the Lordship of Christ to avoid alcohol altogether. Don't flirt with it, sample it, or be pressured into drinking it.

The horror stories about what alcohol does involve people just like you. No injury was intended. No plan was there to use a car as a death instrument. Nobody meant to become an alcoholic. Innocent "experimenters" or "social drinkers" too often become victims to alcohol. Worse still, they victimize others under its influence.

Let's go back to the four "Guidelines About Right and Wrong" we established in Chapter One and apply them to our topic in hope of arriving at a responsible position for Christians to take on this matter.

First, are there **explicit prohibitions** in the Bible? There are certainly a great many which condemn *alcohol abuse* (i.e., drunkenness). "Do not get drunk on wine, which leads to debauchery" (Eph. 5:18). Drunkenness is named among the "works of the flesh" which will cause one to miss the kingdom of God (Gal. 5:21; cf. 1 Cor. 5:11; 6:10).

"Ah," someone says, but those verses relate to *drunkenness*. They don't prohibit drinking in moderation." That's right. The problem is, however, that no one knows when taking his or her first drink whether alcohol is going to become a compulsive element of his or her life. Would you fly Smash Up Airlines if you knew that one of every ten of its flights crashed? Yet there is a one-in-ten chance that every person who drinks alcoholic beverages will become an alcoholic. Good judgment would sound a warning here against starting on a path that so many have been unable to negotiate.

Total abstinence is something which must be defended on a basis other than explicit statements. The second guideline we settled on earlier seems to nail it down.

Second, what **general principles from Scripture** relate to our topic? We have already dealt with one of the most important ones by bringing up Paul's statements in 1 Corinthians 6:12-13. Let's pursue a couple of others which are important, too.

You are created in the image of God, and God's will for you is that you be "conformed to the likeness of his Son"

(Rom. 8:29). I have never met anyone who would defend drinking in moderation on the basis of its ability to make him or her more Christ-like.

The Bible also teaches that your body is a temple of the indwelling Spirit of God (1 Cor. 6:19-20). From what medical science has been able to tell us about the generally negative effects of alcohol on the human body, it seems unlikely that one could make a very strong case for the use of alcohol as an enhancement of your body's strength and vitality.

Third, would drinking harm your **Christian influence?** To the spiritually sensitive mind of the apostle Paul, this seems to have been a most important principle about drinking alcoholic beverages at Corinth. He didn't appeal to a "Thou shalt not ..." to prohibit it, but he did appeal to a principle of concern for how one's actions influence other people. He wrote: "It is better not to eat meat or drink wine or to do anything else that will cause your brother to fall" (Rom. 14:21). A big issue in Paul's day was the eating of meat which had been offered to idols. He counseled Christians at Rome and Corinth (cf. 1 Cor. 10:31-33) to the effect that although eating such meat was not wrong of itself, it would not be best and helpful for the church. He also referred to drinking wine in the same context. What does that say about my responsibility to the body of Christ?

Even if someone knows from experience that he or she can drink moderately without becoming an alcoholic, the good of others who could be influenced to drink and be harmed by alcohol would prohibit it. "Nobody should seek his own good, but the good of others" (1 Cor. 10:24).

Philosophers call that the Principle of Universalizability — always act in such a way that whatever you do could be employed as a general rule that all people could follow. Christians call it the "Golden Rule." Set the sort of example for others that they will always be safe in following. Drinking alcoholic beverages just doesn't fit well with such a commitment.

Fourth, the **advice of the best people you know** would be consistently — if not unanimously — against the use of alcohol as a social beverage.

Didn't Jesus Drink Wine?

Someone will always raise the question, "But didn't Jesus drink wine? What does that do to your case for total abstinence?"

The "wine" used in Jesus' day was very different in nature from what we refer to under the same term. Robert Stein published an excellent article a few years back ["Wine-Drinking in New Testament Times," *Christianity Today* (June 20, 1975): 923-925] which gives extensive documentation from both Jewish literature and Greek writers of the New Testament period concerning the wine people drank. It was considerably lower in alcohol content than today's distilled spirits and was mixed with water in a ratio ranging from two (or more) parts water to one part wine.

People who drank wine in those ancient cultures without mixing it with water or at a one-to-one ratio were considered barbarians who delighted in "strong drink."

Anyone drinking such diluted "wine" would have little problem with inebriation. The alcohol content would be far below the lightest wines or light beers served today. Before you could suffer harm from the slight amount of alcohol it carried, you would be having kidney or bladder problems!

So if by saying "Jesus drank wine" anyone thinks he can justify drinking today's alcoholic beverages, he is mistaken.

When securing pure water was a difficult problem, mixing it with wine was a safety measure against illness (cf. 1 Tim. 5:23). In the same circumstances today, the same measure would be appropriate. Its use as a social beverage in today's society is a very different matter.

As Stein writes: "If the drinking of unmixed wine or even wine mixed in a ratio of one to one with water was frowned upon in ancient times, certainly the drinking of distilled spirits in which the alcoholic content is frequently three to ten times greater would be frowned upon a great deal more."

Conclusion

Earlier in this chapter, the first part of Ephesians 5:18 was quoted. Here is the verse in its entirety: "Do not get drunk

34

on wine, which leads to debauchery. Instead, be filled with the Spirit."

It seems self-evident that the more one is drawn to, uses, and comes under the influence of intoxicating beverages, the less and less place there is for the Spirit of God and his beautiful productivity in that individual's life. On the other hand, the more one comes to be filled with the Spirit and to bear the fruit of the Spirit in his life, the less tolerance he can have for alcoholic beverages in his mind, attitudes, and behavior. After all, "self-control" is a fruit of the Spirit of God in a believer's life (cf. Gal. 5:22-23).

Society is waking up to the dangers of alcohol. It is being recognized as the number one drug problem in America. The increased interest in physical fitness is moving some away from drinking.

Some sports arenas are curtailing beer sales. Several baseball parks, for example, sell no beer after the seventh inning; a few even have designated seating areas where no beer can be sold or carried in by fans at any point during the game.

There are periodic attempts made to eliminate television advertising of alcoholic beverages. A researcher at Michigan State University in East Lansing has found that the average teen-ager in America gets a dose of approximately 1,000 ads for beer, wine, and hard liquor from TV, radio, and magazines. His research also showed that young people who saw that advertising for alcohol drank 10 to 20 percent more than those who saw fewer than 1,000 ads per year.

Lobbying efforts of groups such as Mothers Against Drunk Driving (MADD) have been responsible for much tougher drunk-driving laws in practically every state.

Concerned high school and college students who have seen friends crippled or killed because of alcohol have started their own movements to promote abstinence. Students Against Drunk Driving (SADD) is now a national organization with chapters from coast to coast. Maybe you should begin one in your city.

If you or a friend of yours needs help in dealing with alcohol, talk with your parents, your preacher or Bible class teacher, or a trusted friend and ask him or her to help. Then go together to get in touch with Alcoholics Anonymous (AA), CareUnit, or a similar group in your area which specializes in helping people who have a drinking problem. The God of all grace will provide the daily strength it takes to conquer the problem.

4 / The Drug Culture

She spent $100,000 on drugs in 1982 — $80,000 in the last six months of that year. At five feet four inches tall, her weight dropped to 80 pounds. She stole, hustled on the streets as a prostitute, and filched from her drug-using associates. Today both her body and mind are scarred, but she has been off drugs for eighteen months. It all started in a restroom of a nice restaurant in Aspen, Colorado. A girl dipped her fingernail in a vial and shoved it up her nose. It was her first snort of cocaine and the beginning of nearly a decade of drug experiences that took her through Quaaludes to syringes and back to sanity again. In her words, she's still making it "one day at a time."

Johnny is 30 now. An ex-abuser who started doing drugs at 15 and got straight two years ago, he is trying to help get others away from the addiction which almost cost him his life. "I was a garbage-can addict," he says. "I wasn't choosy. I took pills, drank like a fish, used hallucinogens, did cocaine. I would carry a small aspirin box which contained all the pills I needed, according to how I wanted to feel."

There's good news and bad news about the drug culture in America as we approach the twenty-first century.

The *bad news* is this: Illicit drug use per capita in the United States exceeds that of any other industrial nation in the world. This country has approximately 500,000 heroin addicts, more than 57 million Americans age 12 or older have

37

tried marijuana at least once, and nearly 25 million admit to having experimented with cocaine. Crack, a relatively cheap nugget form of cocaine which is smoked rather than snorted, is even more rapidly addictive and dangerous than cocaine. It is available everywhere.

The *good news* is this: There appears to have been a peaking, a leveling off, and the beginning of a downward trend in drug use within the past few years. For example, government statistics compiled in 1978 indicated that a staggering 10 percent of all high school seniors smoked marijuana daily; in 1986, that percentage had dropped by half.

Law enforcement personnel are frustrated. They admit the traffic in marijuana, cocaine, crack, and "designer" drugs is beyond their ability to control. Although record amounts are being interdicted and destroyed, the overall supply continues to grow. Finding pot or coke is no more difficult in most places than buying a six-pack of beer after the bars close.

We have a strange history regarding drug use in this country. President Ulysses Grant used cocaine in his last years on the advice of Samuel Clemens, better known as Mark Twain. The president of the American Philosophical Society wrote in 1868 to praise opium; under its influence, he asserted, "the intellectual and imaginative faculties are raised to the highest point compatible with individual capacity." In the latter part of the nineteenth century, Coca Cola was a smash hit on the beverage market — bottled with cocaine in its original formula.

A backlash against drug abuse and addiction in the 1920s drove opium and cocaine underground. At about the same time, marijuana began to appear in the country. It, too, was looked upon with horror. A 1936 movie called *Reefer Madness* warned against the "killer weed" which led to insanity and suicide. Drugs were on the fringes of our society through the 1950s.

In the 1960s came Timothy Leary, *Easy Rider,* Haight-Ashbury, and Woodstock. Though illegal, marijuana, LSD, and a variety of other drugs became highly visible.

Even popular TV shows such as Johnny Carson's "Tonight

Show" and "Saturday Night Live" were notorious for drug jokes in the 1970s which treated the use of illegal substances lightly. The networks cracked down on Carson and sponsored public-service announcements by network stars and athletes against drug use, but syndicated episodes of "Saturday Night Live" made before the tightening up policy are re-run in the early evening (when many small children watch TV) in several major cities.

Cheech and Chong movies are virtual commercials for marijuana. Even the more respectable movie *9 to 5,* which has been shown on network television now, includes a marijuana scene. In music, lyrics in a number of songs — especially those of the hard-rock culture — gloried in the "fun" of doing drugs.

On the other hand, a two-part series on drug abuse called "The Chemical People" was narrated by Nancy Reagan on PBS. A powerful NBC movie, *Cocaine: One Man's Seduction,* portrayed the ravages of the drug on a middle-aged real estate salesman. "Diff'rent Strokes" did an episode aimed at pre-teens with an antidrug theme. More programming and public service spots of this sort appear to be the wave of the future.

Perhaps even more effective have been the testimonials of public figures, entertainers, and athletes about their experiences with drugs. In 1978, former First Lady Betty Ford announced that she was entering a hospital to get help in dealing with her dependency on alcohol and pain killers. Jason Robards, Daniel Travanti, Johnny Cash, Darrell Porter, E.J. Junior, Larry Gatlin, and many others have told their stories to the public. At the same time, universities, amateur and professional athletic associations, and the courts have begun coming down hard on drug offenders.

The Primary Drug Threats

From the previous chapter, remember that **alcohol** is the number one drug of abuse in this country. At the same time, very few people who use alcohol with any frequency remain "pure" in their chemical choices. The use of alcohol tends to pave the way to the use of other drugs.

"Polyabuse" is a word now being used in the vocabularies of rehabilitation experts. Most people who become addicted to drugs are hooked on a combination of them. School officials and law enforcement authorities meet a strange reaction among parents of young alcohol abusers. Calling home or work to reach the parents of a kid who is drunk, they are sometimes met with a sigh of relief. "Whew," says the parent, "I'm glad it was a beer party. I was afraid he'd been using drugs!" Adults really can be naive.

Since Chapter Three dealt with alcohol, this one will concentrate on two other drugs most commonly used among teen-agers today: marijuana and cocaine. (As much could be said about cigarette smoking, but only incidental references will be made to it.)

Marijuana is not the "innocent weed" its promoters would have you think it is. Contrary to the T-shirt message "A Friend With Weed is a Friend Indeed," the facts tell a different story.

A 22-member study committee of the National Academy of Sciences spent 15 months analyzing 1,000 scientific studies of the health effects associated with marijuana. The following facts are gleaned from its 188-page report.

The principal active element in marijuana is delta-9-tetrahydrocannabinol (THC). It is known to impair motor coordination, hamper short-term memory, slow learning, and produce distortions of judgment. Dr. Charles O'Brien of the University of Pennsylvania School of Medicine and a member of the committee says, "There's no way a student's brain can function normally when he uses marijuana daily."

THC has been shown to damage the liver, lungs, and body fat cells — as well as the brain. At least half the original dose of THC remains in the body five to seven days after smoking marijuana. It can take up to a month for it to leave the body. If smoked regularly, the substance accumulates.

The committee hopes that medically beneficial uses of marijuana and its derivatives may be found for treating glaucoma, asthma, and the nausea and vomiting associated with chemotherapy in cancer patients.

The Lung Association has recently presented the following additional information about hazardous ingredients other than THC found in marijuana. It has also noted that *the same chemicals are present in tobacco.* (1) Hydrocyanic Acid is the chemical used to execute criminals in California's gas chambers and is linked to chronic bronchitis. An average tobacco cigarette contains 498 micrograms; a marijuana cigarette has 532 micrograms. (2) Acetaldehyde is a lung irritant known to be connected to emphysema. An average tobacco cigarette contains 980 micrograms; a marijuana cigarette, 1,200 micrograms. (3) Benzanthracene is a carcinogen linked to lung cancer. An average tobacco cigarette contains 43 nanograms; an average marijuana cigarette, 75 nanograms. (4) Benzopyrene is another carcinogen tied to lung cancer in humans. The average tobacco cigarette contains 22.1 nanograms, an average marijuana cigarette, 31 nanograms.

Even though the "good news" is that pot use is declining among young people, a darker side of that fact is that there is an increase in the potency of the marijuana being distributed. Richard Grimes, Educational Development Director of the Lung Association, notes, "There's also a decrease in the age of first use, so kids are smoking marijuana when their bodies are most vulnerable. Marijuana is hurting their physical development."

Most people know that pot smokers inhale their smoke more deeply and hold their breath longer than cigarette smokers. That sort of a smoking pattern greatly increases exposure to the toxic substances involved.

It is not an innocent drug. Ask Gary. Now 18, he discovered marijuana four years ago. "It became a constant struggle to hold onto the feeling [of being 'high']," he says. So he went on to speed, Quaaludes, cocaine, and LSD until "it was like my brain was fried."

Gary started dealing drugs at age 15. "I'd walk into the bathroom at school and say 'Quaaludes,' and they'd be gone," he says. By the time he was a senior in high school, he was shooting drugs — cocaine, Percodan, anything he could get his hands on. A concerned uncle got involved in Gary's life, got him into a drug rehabilitation program, and is helping him with plans for college.

Cocaine is thought to be used regularly (at least once a month) by four million to five million people in America. Users are diving nose first into coke when medical studies, crime reports, and death stories should be scaring them off. It is the most "fashionable" drug of abuse among the envied wealthy and glamorous people of our society. For every pound of cocaine seized by drug enforcement agents, six sift out into the marketplace. All levels of our society are involved, and huge amounts of money change hands daily.

Cocaine is said to be the strongest natural stimulant on planet Earth. It is derived from coca, which is cultivated as a cash crop in the Andes Mountains of Bolivia (86,000 acres) and Peru (123,000 acres). All but a small fraction of the cocaine destined for the United States goes first to Columbia and then here.

The legal uses of cocaine relate to flavoring for soft drinks and medical use. Processed leaves of the coca plant with the cocaine removed yield the flavoring used in colas; the cocaine extract is used principally for ear, nose, and throat surgery.

Illegal cocaine is sold on the streets as a white powder, usually containing five to ten percent pure cocaine. It is administered by sniffing (usually called "snorting") and by intravenous injection. Its euphoric effects are well known.

Crack is cocaine boiled down into crystalline form that can be smoked. It was first imported from the Bahamas around 1983. It costs so much less than cocaine and is so much more powerful than cocaine that it represents a vicious threat to people of all ages.

Whereas heroin produces a droopy and lazy high, stimulant cocaine is far more in tune with the mood of America as a country of nonstop go-getters. For a blissful 20 or 30 minutes, users have the illusion of being smarter, more competent, sexier, in charge, and better. "With cocaine," says one ex-user, "you're indestructible, perfect, the giant of your dreams."

For cocaine addicts, "free-basing" produces the ultimate high. The active drug is "freed" from its "base," a hydrochloride salt, by dissolving the cocaine and adding chemical catalysts that cause the free-base to separate. Filtered or skimmed off and then dried, the resulting granules are smoked in a small glass water pipe — often filled with rum instead of water. A butane torch or cigarette lighter is used to apply steady heat on the pipe's bowl to vaporize the free base. (Accidents such as the one Richard Pryor had in 1980 are not uncommon during free basing. His rum spilled, ignited, and set his clothes on fire.)

Typical physiological responses to cocaine are increased alertness, euphoria, dilated pupils, increased pulse rate and blood pressure, insomnia, and loss of appetite. An overdose can cause increases in body temperature, hallucinations, convulsions, or even death. The most common cocaine-related ailment is a breakdown of the nasal membrane; it is the least of the user's worries.

We've Been Brainwashed

This generation of Americans has been conditioned to believe that a pill or potion will cure everything from headaches and insomnia to anxiety and body odor. We are the most over-medicated people in the history of the world.

Just think of the advertising lines you hear on a daily basis: "Feel better fast!" "Fall asleep faster!" "You have to grab for all the gusto!" "For the way you live your life today." "For these symptoms of stress that can come from success." All these messages are designed to make us buy a product with the implicit promise of instant change in the way we feel. Small wonder that young and old alike are caught up in the pressure to drink, smoke, swallow, sniff, or inject some magic substance that will do wonders for us!

The ordinary strains and stresses of living are just that — *ordinary*. The expectation of instant release from problems and instant gratification for ourselves is both ridiculous and dangerous.

Then there is the irresponsibility of some in the medical community who cater to these expectations. "Doc, my job is really a hassle," he says. "Maybe you'd better give me something." Or a woman asks for "something for my nerves." If one physician won't write a prescription for a mood-altering drug, another one probably will.

Chemical dependency starts when you begin depending on a drug to do for you what you ought to do for yourself. If you have a crisis with a boyfriend, face it and deal with it; don't reach for a bottle, pill, or needle. If you feel lonely, jittery, and anxious, a snort of coke will not solve the problem; after a few minutes of drug-induced high, you will be back where you began — possibly less able to use your own physical and mental strength because of the drug experience. If you feel guilty over a wrong done to someone, a joint of marijuana may distract you from it briefly; going to that person, apologizing, and rebuilding the relationship can solve it permanently.

The truth of the matter is this simple: There are no chemical solutions for personal, emotional, and spiritual problems. Your life will never be stress-free, and the sooner you realize it the better equipped you will be for living successfully.

Occasionally an individual can benefit from a psychiatrist's use of mood-altering drugs in the early stages of therapy designed to deal with the real problems of that person's life. The best and most successful of psychiatrists, however, are the ones most reluctant to allow their patients to become drug dependent. No hurting individual is wise and disciplined enough to use street drugs in a program of self-administered therapy!

Don't let chemicals become a distraction in your life to keep you from exercising faith, courage, and genuine character in dealing with life. The use of drugs will not make you feel closer to God or your fellow human beings.

Alcoholics Anonymous says about 30 percent of America's population lives by a policy of absolute abstinence from alcohol, cocaine, and other chemical substances. It really is acceptable *not* to drink, smoke, or snort. It is certainly *right* to stay away from bottles and pills, weeds and powders.

Avoiding the Traps

Some people become addicted to drugs while undergoing legitimate medical treatment. Taking large doses of pain-killing medications following an accident or serious surgery can create an unsought dependency. Pharmaceutical companies are working to find non-addicting substances with the useful properties of narcotic drugs. In the meanwhile, physicians are generally very careful to avoid over-medicating patients. But those who begin a life of chemical dependence via this route are a negligible percentage of today's drug culture.

Many more have started down the drug path due to nothing more sinister than *curiosity*. Just wanting to see what the experience is like, some try a chemical substance and have their curiosity satisfied. They walk away and never experiment with it again. But others are not so lucky. They lose control, repeat the experience again and again, and a dependency is created. There is no way to predict what your experience with marijuana, alcohol, or cocaine would produce. The only safe way is to declare yourself unalterably opposed to the whole culture.

The strongest factor at work in pulling teen-agers into drug use is *peer pressure*. Michael D. Newcomb, a research psychologist at UCLA, did a five-year study of 900 young people through 15 junior and senior high schools. When the study was started in 1975, 70 percent of junior high students in the study had already tried alcohol and 30 percent said they had tried marijuana. When it ended in 1980, 80 percent had tried alcohol and 38 percent were committed users; 50 percent had tried marijuana and 28 percent were twice-a-week users. The influence of friends was given as the most common reason for using both.

Christian teens must choose their friends carefully, for "Bad company corrupts good character" (1 Cor. 15:33). On the other hand, you need not be fatalistic about being in a school where a great many people are drinking or using drugs. Light cancels darkness! With the power of God in your life, you can remain free of chemical substances and become a force for good in setting an example which others can follow. You can be light and salt for the sake of your Lord Jesus (cf. Matt. 5:13-16).

Conclusion

Therapists who work with "chemical people" consistently point to the fact that young people with a strong sense of purpose have the best chance of avoiding the drug culture. Such persons don't need crutches, escapes, and artificial highs.

What do the following people have in common? Diane Linkletter, television actress and daughter of Art Linkletter. Judy Garland, singer and actress. Janis Joplin, female rock star. Jimi Hendrix, rock guitarist. Scott Newman, son of actor Paul Newman. John Belushi, comedian. Ronald Roberts, son of evangelist Oral Roberts. David Kennedy, son of the late Senator Robert Kennedy. Len Bias, basketball player. Don Rogers, professional football player. You've figured it out, haven't you? All these people died from drug abuse. What a waste! But drugs will kill anyone without regard to race, religion, color, or social status.

All the people named above hung around with people they thought were "cool" because they did drugs. They paid too high a price for that association. Drugs aren't cool or smart. They take away life — both physical and spiritual. So go a step beyond just saying "No" to drugs; stay away from the people who use them. Live your life in touch with reality, not running from it. Living with Jesus as the Lord of your life will provide the strong sense of purpose you need to avoid copping out with chemicals.

The strength you need for living comes not from chemicals but from the One whose love and grace can give us all we need to face life. "If God is for us, who can be against us? ... No, in all these things we are more than conquerors through him who loved us" (Rom. 8:31b, 37).

5 / Pornography and Behavior

My doorbell rang at 1:45 a.m. Two college students were standing on our front porch, crying. I knew them both to be genuine Christians. After they came in the house, I asked why they were so upset. "We went to see this movie tonight," he began. "It was supposed to be a pretty good film, even though it carried an R rating. Some friends of ours recommended it. We didn't know it had such explicit scenes about sex in it. It got things on our minds, things started happening in the car after we left the theater, and ..." They both began crying again.

Her son was away at basketball camp, so Becky decided to give his room a thorough cleaning. She found clothes behind the bed, tennis shoes and athletic gear strewn on the floor, and a pile of magazines under a sleeping bag in the closet. She was horrified to discover that they were copies of Hustler, Penthouse, *and the like. She sat in her son's room for a long time trying to decide what to do.*

Laws are on the books to protect our environment. If anyone operates a factory which discharges heavy pollutants through its smokestacks or leaves the lid off his garbage can, he may be slapped with a fine or other penalty. A need to protect planet Earth has been recognized, laws with teeth have been placed on the books, and changes have been made.

Pornography is a pollutant, too. But the effective laws which will begin to clean up the mess have yet to be written. Despite local campaigns to stamp out pornography and occasional success stories, it almost appears to be a no-win battle. More of it is being printed and put on film. Erotica is giving way to brutality and sadism. New markets (e.g., cable TV) are open to its agents.

The Warren Court of 1966 restricted the definition of obscenity to materials judged to be "utterly without redeeming social value." That action turned the porn peddlers loose to strew their garbage into everyone's yard, for some "expert" could be found whose discerning eye could find a trace of social value in anything from gang rape to chain saw murders. The Burger Court of 1973 tried to reverse the trend a bit by giving local juries the right to decide what offended and to convict of obscenity when they found that a work, "taken as a whole, lacks serious literary, artistic, political, or scientific value." This was expected to give prosecutors a standard with which they could work effectively.

The sexual revolution which had already taken place in America by 1973 had so altered "community standards" that no really impressive changes in the pornography establishment have been brought about.

It's Everywhere!

An estimated 20,000 adult bookstores and 900 X-rated movie theaters operate in the United States. Direct sale of pornographic materials through the mail has grown to a $3 billion business in this country. Then there's dial-a-porn, a telephone service in which users call a number to hear a sexually explicit message. The Playboy Channel is bounced off a satellite and provided through many cable systems. Videocassette recorders in homes have opened a new market to pornographers, and families trying to rent a G-rated movie to watch at home often have to wade through shelves stocked with hard-core pornography. The president of one videocassette chain estimates that X-rated films account for one-fifth of all video sales.

People in the pornography trade, already an $8 billion to $10 billion annual business, say sales have never been better.

As pornography has become more widespread, its content has changed considerably. Much of it now portrays graphic violence and degradation rather than erotic material. In Orange County, California, two men have been arrested and charged with murdering two teen-aged girls. Authorities say the girls were killed while being photographed in a porn film. It is estimated that there are at least 250 "kiddie porn" magazines on the market. Common themes are sadism, incest, child molestation, rape, and murder. UCLA psychology professor Neil Malamuth, speaks of the increasing "eroticization of violence" in pornography. Beatings, dismemberment, and (as best as can be determined) simulated murder are central to the thin plot.

People who defend the circulation of pornography in our culture cite the 1970 *Report of the Presidential Commission on Obscenity and Pornography* with its conclusion that there is no cause-and-effect relationship between pornography and violence. As Dr. Michael J. Goldstein says, "Pornography was far less explicit and violent when the 1970 study was conducted than it is now." In the 1980s, there is a growing body of research which demonstrates that exposure to violent pornography contributes to a cultural climate in which crimes of aggression against women and children are more acceptable.

A researcher at Virginia Commonwealth University interviewed 114 convicted rapists about their crimes. Diana Scully concluded from her research that the scenes depicted in pornography were recreated in rapists' accounts of their crimes. Two California researchers tell of a rape victim who was told by her attacker, "I seen it all in the movies. You love being beaten ... You know you love it, tell me you love it." The reports go on and on.

Pornography has become, in the language of one of its publishers, "part of the mainstream of American life."

My concern is not only with hard-core pornography but also extends to a subtler form which gets into everyone's life. I will call it "soft-core pornography" to distinguish it from the raunchiest forms of porn. It comes via TV commercials which sell products with sultry voices and suggestive dialogue, advertisements in newspapers and magazines which use nudity to call attention to themselves, best-selling books which throw in pointless tidbits of erotic babble which are unnecessary to the telling of an otherwise good story, television programs which feature violence and perverted sex, and PG movies which splash vivid violence on the neighborhood theater screen.

Take advertising as a case in point. We have long since become accustomed to the sexy sell. Everything from automobiles to razors is sold with an appeal to some sexual theme. In a Calvin Klein ad for underwear, a woman lies sleeping between two men. The three are clad only in Klein's briefest briefs. No caption. Why they are exhausted is left to the reader's imagination. An ad campaign for his Obsession perfume featured one woman and three men. This time there are not even any briefs, and no one was sleeping. The three naked men are kissing the nude woman. At first, even the advertising industry was critical of the Klein format for product promotion. More recently Revlon, Playtex, Levi's, and others have followed the lead into sensuality in advertising.

For the time being, at least, legislative attempts to curb either soft-core or hard-core pornography are proving to be of limited value. Personal conscience and moral indignation will have to do for morally sensitive people what laws will likely never do for our society as a whole.

Does It Really Influence Behavior

Courts and sociologists have been either unable or unwilling to define the word "pornography" with any precision. The word traces to two Greek words: *porne,* meaning prostitute or that which pertains to a prostitute, and *graphe,* which means writing. Thus the word has reference to the depiction of fornication and sexual impurity in words and pictures.

A standard dictionary definition says that pornography is "the depiction of erotic behavior (as in pictures or writing) intended to cause sexual excitement."

One theory about such materials is that they are harmless. Called the **catharsis theory** (or release theory) by its advocates, this view holds that the more pornography a male viewer sees, the less likely he is to commit a sex crime. In other words, the pornography he reads or watches provides a "harmless" outlet for sexual aggression. In the first place, such a theory insults men by assigning an inherent need for sexual violence to them. Furthermore, it says to women and children, "Let us see a few of you being degraded in our fantasies so that others of you will be spared in reality."

A growing body of information is pointing to the link between pornography and the sexual abuse of women and children. A couple of studies have already been cited in this chapter. All of us know that what we see, read, and hear influences the way we behave.

From Jesus Christ to Adolf Hitler, the assumption of mankind has been that an idea communicated through words and pictures is powerful. As one writer has expressed it: "Everyone acknowledges that encouragements to moral conduct and models of exemplary behavior can influence action; why assume that negative encouragements and models are not equally potent?"

Recently it has become fashionable to hear people of influence in America speaking out against violence in television programs, movies, and literature. The argument has been that examples of violence in such media have a negative impact on our society. Such furor was created by the Steven Spielberg movies *Indiana Jones and the Temple of Doom* and *Gremlins* that Hollywood unveiled a new rating known as PG-13. It was designed for movies deemed acceptable for teen-agers but potentially harmful to younger children.

All this smacks a bit of hypocrisy. Are we expected to believe that scenes of brawling, shooting, and torture can adversely influence the behavior of people seeing it but that the fornication, homosexuality, and infidelity displayed in the same media do not? The cuddly-turned-vicious creatures in *Gremlins* or fish-eye soup and insects of *Indiana Jones* might cause pre-teens to have bad dreams. The sexual perversion paraded in Oscar-winning films will more nearly desensitize all of us to tolerate and even share in conduct that the Bible says is immoral.

51

Contrary to the catharsis theory, the **imitator theory** holds that the more exposure people have to pornography the more likely they will be to engage in illicit or deviant sexual behavior. It can hardly be dismissed as a coincidence that the past decade was marked by a rise in *both* pornography sales and crimes of sexual violence.

Both hard-core and soft-core porn communicate several wrong messages about human beings and sexual activity. It encourages people to see others principally in terms of their sexual parts and functions. It depersonalizes sexual contact and reduces it to a mechanistic function divorced from respect and caring. As it becomes more hard-core, it says there is nothing improper about brutalizing women and children — implying even that they deserve and enjoy such treatment.

Pornography *does* influence attitudes and behavior. The "enjoyment" of pornography is the pleasure of seeing a human being used, devalued, and degraded. As one social worker pointed out: "To be against pornography is not to be against sex. It is to be *for* sex — sex between human beings who respect one another's dignity." A Christian would add: "And the will of a Holy God."

Freedom of Expression

Speak against pornography, however, and you will be reminded of the First Amendment and its guarantee of freedom of expression. "You can't have just a little bit of freedom of the press," goes the argument. "If we want the *New York Times* and *Reader's Digest,* we have to allow everything else someone wants to publish — including pornographic books and magazines."

To defend pornography by associating it with freedom of speech and press is an offense to history and reflects a misunderstanding of the movement for human liberty in this country. Writing for the majority in its 1973 ruling on pornography, Chief Justice Warren Burger said the First Amendment was demeaned when men equated "the free and robust exchange of ideas and political debate with commercial exploitation of obscene material." He expressly said that the 1973 decision represented a decision by the majority of the Supreme Court "to isolate 'hard core' pornography from expression protected by the First Amendment." Obscenity is not within the confines of constitutionally protected speech or press.

If anyone accuses Christians of being against freedom of speech in protesting porn at a neighborhood theater or store, we can remind him that the First Amendment gives us the right to declare "Pornography is offensive," "Pornography is degrading to human beings," and "Pornography does not belong in our community."

Women's groups are doing more to protest and challenge the distribution of pornography in our society than anyone else at present. They are taking on the exploiters of women by pressuring newspapers not to carry ads for movies or clubs which feature sexually explicit material. They are talking to store managers and taking their business elsewhere if pornographic books and magazines are not removed. They are doing from a humanistic base what Christians should have been doing from a commitment to biblical ethics.

What the Bible Says

Absurd as it is, appeals are sometimes made to the Bible in an attempt to justify the public parading of nudity and sexual activity. "The Bible says that Adam and Eve were 'naked and unashamed.' Why should we be embarrassed about returning to Eden?"

Yes, Adam and Eve were naked and unashamed in their original, ideal state. Then came the temptation and fall. After their rebellion against God, they experienced for the first time the sense of shame which always accompanies sin. In particular, their shame was evident in their immediate change of view toward their nudity. They realized they were naked and set about to clothe themselves with leaves. When the Lord came to them following their sin, he did not counsel them to remove their clothes in order to recapture their innocence. Genesis 3:21 tells how he made them heavier and more durable clothing from animal skins.

Originally the nakedness of Adam and Eve signified openness and freedom; after sin's advent, it was associated with shame. From that point forward in the Bible, except within the special intimacy of marriage, the exhibition of one's nakedness or the public performance of acts designed to stimulate sexual arousal is regarded as rebellion against God.

In the Sermon on the Mount, Jesus discussed several parts of the Law of Moses. He contrasted the interpretation of those commands with the original intent God had in giving them. Of importance to this study is what he said about the seventh commandment concerning adultery. The rabbis had come to interpret that commandment in a most rigid manner to include only the physical act of unfaithfulness to one's mate in having sex with a third person. Jesus made it clear that one could violate the commandment long before he was in bed with his neighbor's wife. "You have heard that it was said, 'Do not commit adultery.' But I tell you that anyone who looks at a woman lustfully has committed adultery with her in his heart" (Matt. 5:27-28).

One becomes impure before God by virtue of the deliberate stimulation of erotic thoughts, lustful desires, and sexual fantasies. Sensual stories and lurid photographs are designed to create just such thoughts, desires, and fantasies. Even if one's dabbling with pornography did not cause him to commit fornication or rape, he has still sinned against a holy God.

Coming Closer to Home

The people who control what comes into our homes over TV and into our more respectable neighborhood theaters are not always helping Christians deal with the problem of mind-polluting influences. A study done for *Public Opinion* magazine [Linda S. Lichter, S. Robert Lichter, and Stanley Rothman, "Hollywood and America: The Odd Couple," December/ January 1983] turned up some interesting facts.

Interviews with 104 members of the media elite — reporters, editors, script writers, film editors, and television producers — turned up the following: over half refuse to say adultery is wrong; four out of five did not consider homosexual relationships wrong; 51 percent said adultery was not immoral; 97 percent said women should have an unrestricted right to abortion.

Although 93 percent of the people who participated in the survey said they had a religious upbringing, 93 percent of them also said they seldom or never attend religious services now. Forty-five percent no longer claim any religious affiliation whatsoever, and most of the remaining affiliations appear, in the words of the researchers, "to be purely nominal."

Are these people trying to promote their permissive moral attitudes and anti-religious biases via television? "Two out of three believe that TV entertainment should be a major force for social reform," the report said. "According to television's creators, they are not in it just for the money. They also seek to move their audience toward their own vision of the good society."

Is it any wonder that purity of heart is a difficult attainment? Our culture practically worships sex through its visual media. It has created a situation where having "eyes full of adultery" (cf. 2 Pet. 2:14) is portrayed as the norm.

If we are to be serious about living under the Lordship of Jesus, we will have to guard ourselves against the types of assaults against purity of heart which are involved in all forms of pornographic approaches to life and sexuality. Christians will have to discipline ourselves against seeking out such literature or attending such movies or viewing such TV programs. The Christian who feeds on such things cannot maintain his or her spiritual health.

Conclusion

Using our "Guidelines" established in Chapter One, the attitude of a follower of Jesus Christ toward pornography is vividly clear. Though not explicitly condemned in Scripture (for printing presses and X-rated movies just weren't around then), the principles of the Word of God related to pure thoughts as opposed to the preoccupations of lust relate directly to this matter. "Let the words of my mouth and the meditation of my heart be acceptable in thy sight, O Lord, my rock, and my redeemer" (Psa. 19:14).

There is no question, either, about the impact on your Christian influence which involvement with pornographic books and movies would have. How could you speak to someone about Jesus who knew of your own impure heart? And you know that the people you regard as most Christ-like in your environment would not encourage you to feed your heart on such materials.

A Christian teen-ager once told me about a movie she had seen during the previous week and recommended that I take my wife to see it. Having read a review of the movie in *Newsweek,* I asked about the language (which she admitted was terrible) and a reported scene of nudity (which she remembered). She withdrew her recommendation that we go see it, and she then expressed her personal embarrassment over having sat through it without being sensitive enough at the time to be offended by the things I had asked about.

She was not an ungodly person. She had just been hardened to such things without realizing what was happening. Each of us should look to see whether he or she has been conditioned toward tolerance of the sorts of evil identified in this chapter. What about it?

6 / Wholesome Sexuality

He was in his early twenties and had already secured a rather cushy job under a government officer. The wife of his boss was an immoral woman, however, and she began trying in vain to seduce him. Irate over his persistent rejections and devout religious life, she vented her fury by having him arrested and charged with attempted rape. The innocent young man was sent to prison unjustly.

He was wealthy and powerful, the sort of man who is the envy of many. Yet he was also a pious man and known for an exemplary religious life. One day he chanced to see a woman whom he considered stunningly beautiful. He had enough connections to arrange a clandestine meeting with her, and she (perhaps through fear, flattery, or both) responded to his advances and slept with him. She became pregnant by the man. When the affair became known, its repercussions led to the man's personal disgrace and the frustration of his dream to erect a lavish temple to his God.

Do you recognize either or both of the case studies above? They are taken not from recent newspaper accounts but from the Bible. They are summary accounts of events from the lives of Joseph and David. These are only two of many such accounts in Scripture which deal forthrightly with the subject of human sexuality.

There is no book in the world which deals with the subject of sex in a more direct and wholesome manner than the Bible. One entire book of the Word of God is devoted to the presentation of sexual love in proper perspective (i.e., Song of Solomon). Scripture records the virtues and weaknesses of its characters' sexual conduct with unvarnished detail. It sets forth a standard of sexual behavior which is the highest known to mankind, and it reveals the consequences which come to those who challenge that code.

In this chapter on "Wholesome Sexuality," the Bible's teaching about human sexual conduct will be examined. Its positive and practical nature for young people attempting to glorify the Lord Jesus will be demonstrated.

Sex is Wholesome

Many people have been led to think that the Bible presents a totally negative view of sex. Most of us are more familiar with its prohibitions and negative teaching than with its positive counsel on the subject. That is the fault of our poor use of Scripture rather than any fault within the book itself.

Some theologians of the early Christian centuries presented an utterly depressing picture of the place of sex in human experience. Influenced by certain Greek philosophies, they came to regard the human body and its functions as somehow tainted with evil. They developed a theory which holds that sex is a concession to human weakness. Even married people are to have sex only for the sake of begetting children; thus is explained the opposition of some religious groups to birth control, even in countries where there is insufficient food to keep the population alive.

This negative view of human sexuality is known to American history through Puritanism. The old Puritan ethic allowed no public references to sex, and husbands and wives were to tolerate sex only for the sake of procreation. Women were to wear dark clothing and to cover their bodies entirely.

Some very unhealthy attitudes toward sexuality in general and toward women in particular have been fostered under the influence of preachers and theologians. John Chrysostom, a famous preacher from the fourth Christian century, said: "Woman is a necessary evil, a national temptation, a desirable calamity, a domestic peril, a deadly fascination, and a painted ill." Martin Luther (1483-1546) wrote:

58

"If a woman becomes weary, or at last dead from childbearing, that matters not; she is there to do it."

Chrysostom and Luther "proved" their points from Scripture — allowing a thick layer of culture and tradition to determine their interpretations. Maybe you have heard people who still hold women in such low esteem and who regard sex as something shameful.

Such attitudes are unhealthy and ungodly.

It is not surprising that the sexual excesses of recent times have occurred, for extremes generate opposite extremes. Parents, preachers, and Bible class teachers can be guilty of creating wrong impressions toward sexuality by mishandling the questions of small children or with their uneasiness in discussing the subject when the need arises.

It is right to condemn immoral sex, but it is wrong to create an aversion to the subject. When Christians approach the subject of human sexuality from the perspective of Puritanism rather than that of the Bible, they may very well create mystery around the subject, drive young people to wrong sources for their information about sex, and even contribute to problems in sexual adjustment within the marriages of people under their influence.
within the marriages of people under their influence.

God created the race male and female. When he placed the first man and woman together in Eden, he indicated that their sexual union was to be an important part of the total oneness he desired for them. Quoting the Old Testament record with approval, Jesus said it was heaven's will that husband and wife be "one flesh" in marriage (Matt. 19:5; cf. Gen. 2:24).

That there is nothing unholy about the sexual relationship within marriage is evident from passages such as this: "Marriage should be honored by all, and the marriage bed kept pure, for God will judge the adulterer and all the sexually immoral" (Heb. 13:4). Thus the Holy Spirit made it plain that sex within marriage is wholesome, beautiful, and good. At the same time, he has made it plain that sex outside marriage is degrading, ugly, and sinful. There is a difference between *love* and *lust.*

59

Sex in marriage has been ordained of God as a means by which a man and woman can express their love and commitment to one another. Sex is not only for the begetting of children but is also for the delight of two people in each other as companions.

It is right for Christian teens to look forward to the time when they will be able to experience this pleasure with a husband or wife. Not to wait until marriage for the experience is not only to rebel against the will of God but is also to spoil the joy which could have come with sexual experience. People who experiment with sex before marriage cannot appreciate it, for the God who created us had made it inevitable that feelings of shame and guilt will spoil the experience for them.

It is not wrong for you to feel sexual stirrings during your teen years. It is a natural part of growth. While you are in your teen-age years, your body begins manufacturing hormones which create sexual sensations beyond your ability to change; something you see or hear by chance may excite a sensuous feeling. These things are not under your control and are *not* evil. It *is* wrong, however, to excite sexual feelings deliberately and to exploit them. Pornography, masturbation, petting, and the like have no place in the life of a young man or woman who is attempting to maintain purity under Christ's Lordship.

Remember that purity is not the absence or denial of passion. It is the proper directing and ordering of that passion. Remember also that sexuality is only one aspect of your total personality, and people whose attraction to and use for each other involves sexual desire as the primary element do not have an adequate basis for a permanent relationship.

Abusing Sexuality

Many young people are abusing their sexuality. There is a great deal of confusion among teens about what is normal, right, and expected. Some are given too little moral guidance and too much freedom. Some don't plan to become sexually active before marriage; it just happens.

It was during a party at a friend's house that 16-year-old Brad had his first sexual experience. The friend's parents were away from home, and there were several beers passed around. An older boy had brought condoms. "The goal every time you go out with a girl is to get her in bed," he said. "Having sex is what it's all about around here. All the guys brag about who they've been with. I hate to admit it, but so do I."

The statistics about sexual activity among teen-agers are pretty shocking. Every year, one million adolescent girls become pregnant. About 500,000 teen-agers actually become mothers every year, with the rest of the pregnancies ending in abortions or miscarriages. One-third of all abortions performed every year in the United States are done on teen-age girls. Almost 60 percent of teen births are out of wedlock, compared with 15 percent in 1960. The consensus about sex among teens is that "everybody's doing it." Even among teen-agers who say they have not had intercourse, most believe their friends have.

Events of the last few years seem to be slowing down the involvement of people in their 20s and 30s in casual sex. Most sociologists believe the sexual practices of adolescents will also be altered and become more cautious. Principally, the new conservatism about sexual behavior focuses on sexually transmitted diseases (STDs). According to the Centers for Disease Control, STDs infect an average of 33,000 per day. That totals 12 million cases per year — up from four million in 1980. You may have heard about some of the following: syphilis, trichomoniasis, genital herpes, gonorrhea, chlamydia. You have certainly heard about the most frightening of all the STDs. It is called acquired immune deficiency syndrome, AIDS for short.

AIDS damages the body's immune system, leaving its victims without a defense against a host of serious diseases. New bits of data are published in newspapers daily. It is the most frightening disease modern man has yet encountered, and health authorities believe its proportions will be nothing short of epidemic.

But *fear* will not be sufficient to reestablish sexual chastity. There have been brief returns to sexual conservatism over the centuries in the face of disease epidemics. They have not lasted. The brief impact of fear will not be sufficient to make people moral.

Scare tactics will not produce real and lasting change. We will have to do something more fundamental. We will have to reexamine the whole issue of morality and its relationship to God. We will have to challenge our generation to reconsider the moral absolutes in Scripture.

The truth is that our sex-saturated culture is actually conservative compared to the world into which Christianity was born.

Fornication was so common in the first-century world that the New Testament bristles with specific prohibitions of the sin (cf. Acts 15:20; 1 Cor. 5:1-11; Gal. 5:19-21; Eph. 5:3). No one can think himself or herself a disciple of Jesus Christ who is defying his call to moral purity. The marvelous truth of the New Testament is that the Son of God forgives sexual sins, but he forgives with the demand, "Go now and leave your life of sin" (John 8:11).

Steps Toward Purity

First, remember that **sexual misconduct is an offense against God.** For a Christian, it just isn't true that "It's my life and I can do with it as I please." We have been purchased unto God by the blood of Jesus.

Looking around you at the six-is-where-it's-at attitude of your peers, you are tempted to view fornication one way. Looking beyond the moment to consider the person-to-person relationship you have with Christ, you view the temptation another way. Remember what kept Joseph from jumping in bed with Potiphar's wife? "How then could I do such a wicked thing and *sin against God?*" he said to her. "And though she spoke to Joseph day after day, he refused to go to bed with her or even be with her" (Gen. 39:9-10).

Second, keep in mind that **your body is pledged to God as an "instrument of righteousness."** When you were baptized, you were united with Christ's death and raised to live a new life (Rom. 6:4). Henceforth you are to "count yourselves dead to sin but alive to God in Christ Jesus" (Rom. 6:11). And just what does that mean? Here is the explanation in Paul's own words: "Therefore, do not let sin reign in your mortal body so that you obey its evil desires. Do not offer the parts of your body to sin, as instruments of wickedness, but rather offer yourselves to God, as those who have returned from death to life; and offer the parts of your body to him as instruments of righteousness" (Rom. 6:12-13).

To Christians living in the wicked environment of Corinth, Paul wrote: "Flee from sexual immorality. All other sins a man commits are outside his body, but he who sins sexually sins against his own body" (1 Cor. 6:18). Other sins may be committed impersonally and anonymously — but not fornication.

Third, remember that **fornication is a sin against your own personality.** Honor, self-respect, and reputation are not small items. Failing to keep your sexual passions under restraint is a sure way to lose all three.

Your virginity can be given only once in a lifetime. Not to place that unique event in the context of love, commitment, and Christian marriage is to sell yourself short and to spoil what should be a beautiful event. I repeat: *sexual sin is not unpardonable, but it leaves a special sense of guilt that can remain as a barrier to spiritual peace for a lifetime.*

Conclusion

The "playboy/playgirl philosophy" is a dead-end approach to life, ethics, and responsibility. It creates a world in which self-gratification becomes an end in itself. It ignores the harsh realities of guilt, unwanted babies, and heartache. It has no place for commitment, respect, or God.

A Christian view of life and love presents *wholesome sexuality* as an alternative.

Beth is 17 and plans not to have sex until her honeymoon. "I want to wait until I get married to have sex," she says. "That is something you should share with someone you'll be with the rest of your life. I just don't see how girls can go from guy to guy. I'm glad I am a Christian and have had the teaching of my Savior to keep me from making the awful mistake some of my friends have made." That's an attitude Beth can live with — in personal good conscience and with her relationship with Jesus uncompromised.

7 / If the Music is Off-Key

We sat together in the den. He was nervous and said he hadn't been able to sleep much for several nights. When he called me, there was a note of panic in his voice. He played in the band of a successful crossover artist who moved from country to rock and had placed two singles on the national top-ten charts within six months. Home for a few weeks for a break between road tours and rehearsal of some new material, he was having real struggles with his conscience. This is what he had always dreamed of doing, but the liquor, drugs, and sex of the fast lane in rock music were both frightening and tempting to him. He just had to talk with somebody and figure out what to do.

He was the top-rated personality of the radio market in a city of 800,000 people. He was also a Christian. "I played [rock music] on my show until I just couldn't live with it any longer. The lyrics were so blatantly sexual and got way beyond my tolerance level. My boss thought I was crazy, but it was an easy decision for me to make. I just resigned."

The true case studies above have probably prejudiced some who will read this chapter against anything that lies ahead. Let me see if I can counter some of that negative and defensive feeling.

I enjoy music of practically all varieties. The point of this chapter is not to put it down. I grew up to the sounds of Elvis, the Beatles, Simon and Garfunkel, and Elton John.

My tastes now run more to Neil Diamond, Anne Murray, and Lionel Richie, but I also listen to Restless Heart, Toto, and Atlantic Starr.

Although I didn't grow up listening to country music, living in Nashville for the past decade has exposed me to it. Although a purist would probably take exception to my choices, I like listening to Alabama, the Oak Ridge Boys, and Willie Nelson.

You're right. Mine is not a sophisticated musical palate. I don't know anything about jazz or classical music. There are some powerful messages in some of the contemporary Christian music I have heard. Neither tone-deaf nor talented, there is something of the Heinz 57 touch to my musical tastes.

There's no way, then, that I can launch into a tirade against the music of your culture. God hasn't decreed that rock is wrong and classical is right. It is certainly not my place to decide for you what songs you can and cannot hear, perform, or see on videos. My purpose is simply to point out that Christian living in a culture such as ours requires young people to make responsible and informed choices. I don't have to tell you that some of today's music is tasteless, bizarre, and vulgar. Somewhere between Motley Crue and Muzak, surely there is a place where someone living under the Lordship of Jesus Christ can find music to enjoy.

The Sounds of Music

Music is neither good nor bad of itself. It is comparable to painting, sculpture, or writing in that it is an *art form* which can be used for evil or for good.

There are over 500 specific references to music in the Bible. One book of the Bible (i.e., Psalms) is a collection of song lyrics used to praise God in Jewish worship first and then later in Christian assemblies. Texts of songs are interspersed throughout the Word of God (cf. Luke 1:46-55; 1 Tim. 3:16b; Phil. 2:6-11). The use of music is a required part of worship to our God, for we are commanded to "sing psalms, hymns and spiritual songs with gratitude in your hearts to God" (Col. 3:16).

This is not to say that music should be used only in the context of worship. Composing and performing music is a legitimate form of artistic expression. It is the use of a gift or talent that is God-given.

Some of the music which has been produced by modern artists rises far above the level of discordant sound and obscene lyrics. Christian young people should not be afraid to pluck the diamonds out of the desert. Few of us avoid art galleries or museums because of the occasional piece of vulgar painting; we look for, find, and relish the truly beautiful works among the total collection. The same thing can be done with modern music. Without accepting everything that is offered us, we can be discerning and learn to appreciate the good which is found.

Extreme attitudes toward modern music are reflected in the following quotations. Both of the people quoted are responding to the same question about how rock music in general has affected American culture. One writer speaks totally negatively and says: "Rock permeates virtually every aspect of American life. It has popularized drug usage, promiscuity, sensualism, ugliness, filthy language." Another speaks glowingly and says: "Without rock music we'd be in serious trouble as a culture, for we would have on our hands a generation of young people without any means of expression yet with incredible personal needs for release. It gives young people permission to be young, to act young, to enjoy their youth and savor it before moving on."

Again, as in so many cases, the truth lies somewhere between the two extremes.

A mark of spiritual maturity is the ability to distinguish good from evil and to have the strength of character to choose the former and reject the latter. In the life of a child of God, Jesus is the Lord of Music. He expects us to evaluate our music — as well as our literature, friendships, use of money, etc. — in light of the revelation of the divine will found in the Word of God.

On the one hand, parents and older Christians should not rush to condemn all of today's music simply because it is not the music they knew growing up. There is no reason to label all of it "evil" simply because they don't like it or because it is played too loudly for their sensitive ears. On the other hand, young Christians should not defend everything in the culture of modern music just because it is associated with their generation. Good judgment and discernment are better than emotionalism and prejudice.

It's Big Business

The recorded-music industry was once a relatively minor enterprise. It has emerged as second only to television in the entertainment field. Record companies or their parent corporations are traded in the stock market, and the industry is now a multi-billion-dollar enterprise. More money in the hands of young people, more leisure time, and slick promotion of an artist or group have combined to make it possible.

Recording artists have become some of the nation's biggest idols. From Elvis through the Beatles to Prince, the hair, clothing, and general lifestyle of rock stars are imitated by their admirers.

Some sociologists are convinced that rock music is the strongest of all social influences on tens of thousands of American young people — especially those without close ties to the traditional sources of guidance such as family and church.

One 19-year-old from Fresno, California, says: "I think MTV [the cable music station] is a particular problem. Everything is portrayed in such a glamorous light and is so artsy that if you spend a lot of time with it, which teen-agers do, you can get caught up in the music and the haircuts and the fashions. It becomes the focus of kids' lives, not just their recreation."

A musical group under contract to a major record company can go from unknowns to superstars in a matter of months. To have that happen and to get in on the huge money involved is the consuming dream of thousands of people in this country.

Music Says Something

The ethical problem with some of today's music is not so much the fashions and hairdos it inspires or the big money it generates for a few and the false illusions for many others. It has to do with the anti-Christian message it sometimes carries.

In 1982 several newspaper headlines were made by individuals claiming to find a phenomenon called "back masking" on some popular songs. It was claimed that subliminal messages were hidden in songs which could be "unmasked" by tape recording the records and then playing the tapes backwards. Queen's hit single "Another One Bites the Dust" was supposed to carry the hidden phrase "Start to smoke marijuana"; Led Zeppelin's album *Stairway to Heaven* was alleged to carry such phrases as "Satan is lord," "Jesus betrayed us," and "I will sing because I live with Satan."

For what it may be worth, my personal opinion is that the furor over "back masking" was a tempest in a teapot. If such messages actually existed, there is certainly no good reason for thinking that they reached or influenced anyone's consciousness. The subliminal impact of backward phrases is zero insofar as anyone can tell.

The real moral threat of any music lies in (1) its direct message which is preached to the hearers and (2) the indirect impact which comes to admirers who want to imitate its performers' real or imagined lifestyles.

The late 1970s and early 1980s witnessed a phenomenal invasion of Satanism and the occult into rock music. Groups such as Black Sabbath, AC/DC, Led Zeppelin, Blue Oyster Cult, and the Rolling Stones became promoters of occultism. For example, the cover of AC/DC's *Highway to Hell* album carried the face of the lead singer with devil's horns on his head and a pentagram (i.e., five-sided star used in witchcraft ceremonies) around his neck. The lyrics of the lead song proclaim: "Nobody's gonna mess me around ... Hey, Satan, payin' my dues ... I'm on the highway to hell, highway to hell." The Rolling Stones did a song entitled

"Sympathy for the Devil" in which the police are depicted as criminals and God as the devil.

The preoccupation of many of the same groups seems to center on behavior as outrageous as their music. On the inside cover of their *Minute by Minute* album, the Doobie Brothers display a partially smoked joint of marijuana, a "doobie." On-stage drinking and/or drug use encourages the same among people at their concerts. Police have predictable problems when such groups perform in any city. Groups such as Queen and Boy George and the Culture Club parade a homosexual image. Do these things influence behavior? They give the impression that flaunting immorality is avant-garde rather than reprehensible behavior. The impact is powerful and predictable.

The crest of the Satanism-occult wave in rock seems to have passed now. Even some of the more overt lyrics encouraging drug use have been toned down, for this society has seen too much harm come from drugs for city fathers to tolerate the use of public auditoriums for groups who will come in and evangelize for the drug culture. But the constant emphasis on sex has not diminished. In fact, as occultism and drugs have faded, sensuality has been emphasized all the more.

Even the more mainline performers have gotten into the sex theme. Olivia Newton-John says she was tired of being seen as a goody-goody, so she sang "Let's Get Physical." The album cover carries a variety of sensual poses that would not give the impression of a goody-goody!

Rock star Prince has been phenomenally successful in selling records. The sound track to *Purple Rain* sold 17 million copies worldwide. He has also established himself as a vulgar libertine who is willing to attack Christian values. Even though he dedicates his albums to God, his performances are notorious for his erotic lyrics and obscene behavior on the concert stage. His song "Sister" describes incest as "everything it's said to be." His "Darling Nikki" begins: "I knew a girl named Nikki/ I guess you could say she was a sex fiend / I met her in a hotel lobby / masturbating with a magazine." Prince went too far for toleration in many quarters with his 1985 song "Erotic City." Distinct and repeated slang references to the sex act in it caused many disc jockeys and station managers to refuse to play it.

Frequent play of "Erotic City" on Cleveland radio stations led the Cleveland City Council to pass a resolution requesting stations to refrain from playing recordings with profanity or sexually explicit lyrics. It passed without opposition. A disc jockey in Los Angeles started a "Prince Makes Me Puke" campaign and was shocked at the thousands of orders that flooded his station for T-shirts emblazoned with the slogan.

To be fair in the matter, parents who may try to urge their children away from rock music to country-western don't have a great deal more to recommend. Music from this category often depicts hard-drinking men, husbands and wives who cheat on each other, one-night stands, divorce, and depression. The Kendalls made money by glamorizing illicit sex in "Heaven's Just a Sin Away." Kenny Rogers, among the hottest male singers of the past several years, has recorded some good music. He has also sung "Scarlet Fever," a song about a "nightclub teaser" who was the object of his nightly fantasies; he borders on kiddie porn by singing "She looked 25, but I was told she was just 16." Barbara Mandrell, an energetic and talented lady who has established herself as an entertainment phenomenon, was willing to sing these words to a married man: "If loving you is wrong, I don't want to be right."

MTV is essentially a rock music station that you can watch. Started by Warner Amex Satellite Entertainment Company in 1981, it transmits rock videos seven days a week, 24 hours a day. Well over 2,000 cable systems carry it. What was once suggested or explicitly said in words is now also displayed visually in three-minute video productions. The *New York Times* has stated: "After all, adolescent sexual fantasies are what many rock numbers — and therefore rock videos — are all about."

The video for "Hurts So Good" features a writhing, chain-bound woman. Vignettes of violence and destruction are commonplace. Robert DiMatteo of *Cablevision* magazine described MTV as "a world of youth and erotic possibilities, of situations out of old Hollywood movies, of easy sex, tarnished romance, pretty girls and pretty boys, too."

The task of the Christian in this ocean of records, tapes, and videos is *discernment.* What can you find in the music culture that Jesus likes? He can help you sort through all the elements of your society and make right choices.

Applying Our Standards

Getting back to the "Guidelines About Right and Wrong" identified in Chapter One, it is time to apply them to the subject at hand.

Is there any **explicit command or prohibition** involved? Perhaps. There are certainly no references in Scripture to stereo equipment or MTV. But there are commandments which prohibit using God's name profanely, blaspheming holy things, or glorying in evil. This verse certainly seems relevant: "Do not let any unwholesome talk come out of your mouths, but only what is helpful for building others up according to their needs, that it may benefit those who listen" (Eph. 4:29). Music that entertains and lifts the spirits could be defended from the text just cited; music that attacks Christian values and points to unwholesome things is clearly prohibited. This would mean, for example, that Paul McCartney and Stevie Wonder's "Ebony and Ivory" speaks meaningfully to young people on an important theme to promote understanding and harmony between the black and white races; on the other hand, Loverboy's "Hot Girls in Love" represents another perspective on the nature of human relationships.

Are there **general principles of Scripture** which relate to musical tastes? You might read such passages as 1 Corinthians 10:31 and Philippians 4:8 and reflect on their relevance to the matter. These verses encourage Christians to glorify God in our actions and to focus our hearts on wholesome things. Applied to today's music scene, these passages seem to place a burden of conscience on Christians to be sure that we do not perform, encourage others to perform, or otherwise encourage those who are selling anti-Christian values through their musical messages.

Does one's **influence for Christ** suffer by being involved with modern music? Not necessarily. It depends on the *discernment* you show in your taste. To enjoy music with your friends can be a wholesome recreation and establish communication which can be used for sharing Christ with them. To be involved with music which is tasteless, uses God's name in evil ways, promotes drug use, or glorifies immoral sex is to destroy the possibility of using the same mouth to speak for Jesus.

What of the opinion of the **best Christians you know**? Just try to imagine that man or woman whom you respect most as a Christian listening with you to your records or tapes. Think about asking that person to go with you to the last concert you attended. If feelings of uneasiness or embarrassment arise in these mental exercises, you might want to rethink your tastes.

Conclusion

The music of any generation telegraphs the mental-emotional-spiritual pulse of a significant part of that society. The general spirit of rebellion against God and all that is holy which has invaded our culture is evident in much of its music. This means that a Christian has some sifting and choosing to do.

God has called his people to the difficult and delicate task of redeeming their cultures rather than being squeezed into their mold (Rom. 12:1-2). As bewildering as the task is at times, it is a responsibility that you as a believing young person cannot shun.

Regarding the role of pop music in your spiritual life, you might think of it this way: If the spiritual emphasis of any particular piece of music is off-key with the values you have embraced in your commitment to follow Jesus, just don't play along.

8 / Money Isn't Everything

Harry Monsen, a University of Illinois anatomy professor, calculated that the chemicals remaining in a cremated body were worth $7.28. Another anatomist, Harold Morowitz of Yale University, figured that a live person was worth six million dollars — when hormones and DNA were included. A life-insurance group put a homemaker's value at $1.4 million to show that a woman needs life insurance. Average judicial settlements for survivors of plane-crash victims run something above half a million dollars. Are dollar price tags the only ways we have to determine the value of a life? What of the statement of Christ that one soul is worth more than the whole world?

A great many barriers have fallen to women in the job market. Although there are still a great many inequities, women can enter, compete, and succeed in fields which were typically dominated by men only a few years ago. When her husband died, Mary went to work in real estate and now owned her own company. Her 15-year-old daughter had private school and the best of everything. "Yeah, I've had everything," she said, "except a mother. I wish we could have had less money and more time together. When I need her to be my mother, somebody else needs her as a businesswoman. I always tend to come in second."

It was common for Jews of the first century to bring disputes of all sorts to a rabbi. One day as Jesus was teaching a crowd of thousands, someone in the group interrupted him

75

to request, "Teacher, tell my brother to divide the inheritance with me" (Luke 12:13). Jesus refused to be drawn into the matter. In response to the request, however, he did express his concern with the moral and spiritual implications of what was going on between this man and his brother.

Whether intended as a rebuke to the man asking the question or to his brother, Jesus spoke to say: "Watch out! Be on your guard against all kinds of greed; a man's life does not consist in the abundance of his possessions" (Luke 12:15).

When human beings see nothing beyond this world, we become greedy, covetous, and materialistic. When one of us sees nothing beyond his or her own selfish interests, he may resort to lying, stealing, or murder to get what he wants. Even an otherwise decent and honest person can simply get caught up in the rat race of materialism and burn out as a workaholic.

In the context of the interruption and response in Luke 12, Jesus went on to tell the Parable of the Rich Fool. The man was prosperous but selfish. He thought only of himself in his wealth and disregarded both the needs of poor fellow men and the service of God. "You have plenty of good things laid up for many years," he said to himself. "Take life easy; eat, drink and be merry" (Luke 12:19).

What was the spiritual status of that man in God's eyes? "But God said to him, 'You fool! This very night your life will be demanded from you. Then who will get what you have prepared for yourself?' " (Luke 12:20). After it was too late to do him any good, the man discovered that money isn't everything. Property and cash are not permanent possessions. Because he had put all his energy into material things, he had nothing he could really call his own. His "untimely death" revealed his genuine poverty.

Jesus summed up the meaning of this parable in these words: "This is how it will be with anyone who stores up things for himself but is not rich toward God" (Luke 12:21).

Jesus' story reminds me of a man I knew a few years back. His was a modern Horatio Alger story. Dropping out of college after a year and a half, he went into sales with a manufacturing firm. He was phenomenal at bringing in orders and soon became regional sales director. His meteoric rise continued until the title on his door was "Vice President for Sales" and his annual salary was well into the six-figure range. He drove an expensive sports car, wore custom-tailored suits, and owned a house valued at more than a half-million dollars. He had barely turned 30 and seemed to have it made. Sitting in my office, however, he looked like anything but a winner. He was crying and telling me about his alcoholism and pending divorce. I didn't envy him.

If we are going to address the ethical issues which are really practical in the lives of young people trying to live for Christ today, something must be said about materialism.

What is Materialism?

Materialism is "a preoccupation with or undue stress upon material rather than with intellectual or spiritual things." It is equivalent to what the Bible calls "covetousness" (KJV, ASV, RSV) or "greed" (NIV). It is an obsession with money and the things money can do.

Many of the **dangers of materialism** are evident. Reference has been made already to lying, stealing, and murder. The gambling industry could not exist without greed as a motivating factor. Male and female prostitutes ply their trade for money rather than love. "People who want to get rich fall into temptation and a trap and into many foolish and harmful desires that plunge men into ruin and destruction. For the love of money is a root of all kinds of evil. Some people, eager for money, have wandered from the faith and pierced themselves with many griefs" (1 Tim. 6:9-10).

Some of the dangers of materialism are *subtler*. Some teenagers become snobs because they have cars or clothes that others can't afford. They judge others by where they live or by the pocket money they have. And others choose careers based only on the amount of money they expect those jobs to generate. Isn't that materialism?

Some young people find it easy to get into drugs precisely because they have too much money in their pockets. On the other hand, some teens without much money get into selling drugs for the sake of turning a fast buck.

Some of the people you know have thrown themselves into their careers as if nothing else in life matters for them. They have no free time for themselves, their families, or for God. They can lose their joy for living, develop psychological problems, and become particularly susceptible to diseases such as strokes or heart attacks.

Sometimes young couples go so deeply in debt that, even with two salaries, they cannot make ends meet. So desperate to have a fine house and new car, they strap themselves with money tensions that can mean real trouble in their relationship.

One Bible writer urged his readers to be "free from **the love of money** and be content with what you have" (Heb. 13:5). Paul taught that "godliness with contentment is great gain" (1 Tim. 6:6). Those fortunate enough to be wealthy were counseled "not to be arrogant nor to put their hope in wealth, which is so uncertain, but to put their hope in God" (1 Tim. 6:17). It is much more important to be "rich in good deeds" than in money and to be "generous and willing to share" (1 Tim. 6:18).

Both Jesus and Paul taught that it is more important to use whatever is under your control to honor God and lay up heavenly treasure than to hoard treasures on earth (cf. Matt. 6:19-21; 1 Tim. 6:19).

Money is not sinful of itself, and there is no sin in working hard, investing wisely, and becoming wealthy. *It is not money that is evil but the attaching of too great an importance to it.* Abraham and Job were men of tremendous wealth, yet both of these biblical millionaires were faithful men of God. Lydia was a successful businesswoman who used her wealth to support the ministry of Paul at Philippi (Acts 16:11-15).

Prosperity is a blessing from God. But one who is wealthy must guard against letting that wealth become more important than the Lord Jesus in his life. When the pursuit of this world's goods causes one to neglect the pursuit of heavenly treasure, to hold back liberal gifts from the Lord in order to have more for self, or to compromise faith and moral principle, he or she has become a materialist.

Remember the episode with the Rich Young Ruler? His problem was not that he was either rich or young; it was that he loved his money more than he loved Christ. When it came down to a choice between one or the other, he held to his gold. What are the chances of someone with that attitude going to heaven? Jesus said it would be easier to shove a camel through the eye of a sewing needle! (Luke 18:18-15).

Materialism is a form of **idolatry** (Col. 3:5), for it puts money and the things it can buy in the priority place that God alone deserves in a human life.

Money and Twisted Values

Economic security is one of the major concerns of life. There are many things we need — life's "necessities." There are others things which are nice to have and which we want. Having a job and earning money go with the responsibility of life on planet Earth.

To give you an idea of how much it costs to live, a study released by the Urban Institute in May of 1984 might be helpful. A group of researchers calculated how much it would cost to rear a child. They assumed an average 5.2 percent annual inflation and a family size of two adults and two children. The bill for getting a child to age 18 will be $142,700. If expenses are carried through four years of college, add another $53,000 to $167,300, depending on the school chosen.

Materialism is not the issue when it comes to necessities and a reasonable amount of life's extras. Materialism crosses that acceptable line and begins to judge the worth of a person by the money he has. It confuses human values and puts the highest price tags on the things of least real worth.

For centuries people dreamed of a time when men and women could be freed from constant toil just to stay alive. They envisioned the noble and worthy tasks to which their envied descendants would one day put their hands. They looked to that happy time and contemplated the peace and fulfillment which would be its hallmarks.

Today we live in the time those people dreamed about. Over the past 20 years, the average workweek of an American citizen has dropped from 38.6 hours to 35.3 hours; most

79

people now have more than 120 nonworking days per year. We have become a fun-seeking nation which spends more on sports, recreation, and entertainment than on the defense of our nation. One of every eight dollars spent by American consumers this year will go for leisure activities. Is that what our great-great-grandparents foresaw?

As we have become more affluent, we seem to have proved the truthfulness of an ancient Roman proverb: "Money is like seawater — the more one drinks the thirstier he becomes."

A good case can be made for professional sports as an example of an industry which exhibits confused values by putting the highest price tags on the things of least real value. According to figures compiled by the Major League Players Association, the average salary of a major league baseball player in 1967 was $19,000. By 1976 it was $51,501. By the summer of 1986, the average salary in the big leagues had skyrocketed to $431,521. Fifty-six players were paid one million dollars or more in 1986. In that same calendar year, the average schoolteacher's salary was $25,257.

Boxers have earned five to ten million dollars for a single fight. A surgeon who saves dozens of lives a year with skills that he spent a decade or more to acquire may average $200,000 a year.

A basketball player may make over a million dollars per year. Yet people in the same city where he plays may protest paying firefighters or police officers $22,500 per year.

It is difficult to think that professional athletes — skillful and exciting as they are — invest more time and money in training than physicians or that their performance is more socially beneficial than that of teachers or police officers. Perhaps we have been duped into thinking that "having fun" is more important than anything else. Perhaps the profit-hungry peddlers of entertainment have sold us on the idea that the performers they have packaged and sold us are worth the money they receive.

Can we honestly expect young people to take education seriously when society gives its highest honors to athletes and musicians? Can we expect teen-agers to seek out careers in service to others when the big money is going to entertainers? Can we expect our society to value spiritual qualities above material pursuits when we prioritize the things we do?

Consider what you are looking to as a career goal. Are you focusing on that career primarily because it promises to make you wealthy? There is more to life than money.

From Heaven's Perspective

The world has always thought that happiness and prosperity go hand in hand. Jesus insisted that happiness depends not on what you *have* but on what you *are*. Even if the world reserves its loudest cheers for millionaires who live in mansions and drive limousines, God looks on the heart and praises the meek, the merciful, the pure in heart, and those who bear reproach for his sake.

As people crave success by worldly standards, competition sets in. As competition intensifies, it generates jealously, bitterness, and dishonesty.

The drive to make money has put many people in jobs they end up hating. Dr. Douglas LaBier, a psychoanalyst who spent six years studying how careers affect emotional problems, says flatly that "half of those considered successful by their peers are unhappy."

One's bank account and the cut of his clothes do not determine his standing with God, the stability of his marriage, or the satisfaction he feels at the end of a day. It will be worthwhile for you to keep that in mind as you plan for your future.

God created you in his own image and empowered you to have dominion over this earth and its abundant material wealth. Don't let life turn the tables on you and put you under the domination of wealth. God would have you to love people and use things for their sake. Don't reverse your priorities and wind up loving things so much that you use people for the sake of acquiring them.

Applying the Four Guidelines

Returning again to our "Guidelines" from Chapter One, there are **explicit condemnations of greed** and materialism in the Bible. Several of these texts have been identified in this chapter. Colossians 3:5 is an especially emphatic passage on the topic of covetousness. There is no question of the soul-jeopardizing nature of such a lifestyle.

There are also many **principles of right living** identified in Scripture which are violated by covetousness. For example, Jesus said that no one can serve two masters so opposed to each other as righteousness and greed: "Either he will hate the one and love the other, or he will be devoted to the one and despise the other. You cannot serve both God and Money" (Matt. 6:24). And Paul taught that the meaning of life for a Christian is in seeking things above rather than things of this earth: "Since, then, you have been raised with Christ, set your hearts on things above, where Christ is seated at the right hand of God. Set your minds on things above, not on earthly things" (Col. 3:1-2).

Your **influence for Christ** will be diminished to whatever degree you put money above righteousness in ethics or personal priorities.

And is there any question about the relative value of righteousness to profit in the lives of the **best people** you know? You probably know someone whom you respect for his or her Christian character who is also wealthier than most people. Think about it for a minute and you will probably realize that one reason you respect him or her relates to the way that person uses money to help others instead of keeping things for selfish purposes.

Conclusion

Speaking to a graduating class of McGill University, the English poet Rudyard Kipling advised the graduates not to care too much for money or power or fame. He said: "Someday you will meet a man who cares for none of these things, and then you will know how poor you are."

Jesus Christ was such a person. He gave up heaven, glory, and service by angels to humble himself for our sakes. He washed the feet of his disciples. He offered up his life on the cross. We cannot follow him and be caught up in selfishness.

As you build a life under the Lordship of Jesus, put your trust in the really stable things you cannot lose rather than in life's perishable material things. Put the kingdom of God and his righteousness first in your life, and trust God to provide for you out of his bountiful resources (cf. Matt. 6:33).

9/ Dealing With Racial Prejudice

A group of teen-agers left the building on Saturday to distribute invitations to Vacation Bible School. They noticed that several streets near the church building had been marked off the map and were not to be canvassed. They asked why — suspecting already that they knew the answer. The people living on those streets were mostly black. After talking with the canvass organizer about the matter, they went to every house on every street. They believed the business of the church involves reaching out to all people.

A pretty, three-year-old girl was upset. She went to her father and said, "I want mine to be like that." With amused concern, he tried his best to be sympathetic and to explain. Later he related the whole incident to his wife. They commented that the incident confirmed their belief that racial prejudice is learned rather than instinctive behavior. And what was the issue? The little white girl had been playing with a black girl of the same age. She noticed the difference in skin color and was convinced that she had been cheated!

Old Testament Israel misinterpreted its relationship to Yahweh and to the nations surrounding it. "Now if you obey me fully and keep my covenant," said the Lord, "then out of all nations you will be my treasured possession. Although the whole earth is mine, you will be for me a kingdom of priests and a holy nation" (Ex. 19:5-6).

The selection by grace to be God's chosen people generated smug self-righteousness and bigotry. Instead of serving and enlightening the nations around itself, Israel became cold and aloof. The Gentile was an abomination. His touch was defiled, and on coming from the market an orthodox Jew of the first century was expected to immerse himself to cleanse the defilement which rubbing elbows with Gentiles would have generated. Tacitus, the Roman historian, wrote of the Jews that "among themselves they are inflexibly faithful and ready with charitable aid, but hate all others as enemies. They keep separate from all strangers in eating, sleeping, and matrimonial connections."

There is no Old Testament legislation forbidding normal social contact between Jews and Gentiles. Regulations doing so were formulated by the rabbis and became binding by strength of social custom. The Old Testament book of Jonah shows the breadth of divine love as contrasted with the narrowness of human sentiment. Since the Ninevites were enemies of the Israelites, Jonah did not want them to repent and be spared; he wanted God to destroy them with fire and brimstone. That is why he tried to avoid going there to preach (Jon. 4:2; cf. Jer. 18:5-10).

The apostles and other earliest members of the church of Christ were all Jews and had to deal with the problem of racial prejudice before the gospel could reach to Samaritans and Gentiles. It was no small hurdle to overcome. They were heirs to the strongest racial prejudice history had ever known to that point.

How the Early Church Handled It

For nearly ten years after Pentecost, the gospel was kept almost exclusively among the Jews. A few Samaritan villages had heard the Word of God from men such as Philip, Peter, and John (Acts 8:5, 14, 25). The Gentiles of the larger Roman world, however, remained shut off from the message of salvation in Christ because of Jewish prejudice and racial exclusivism.

The situation began to change when a vision came to Peter which impressed this message on his consciousness: "Do not call anything impure that God has made clean" (Acts 10:15).

The apostle did not fully comprehend the significance of these words until, at the urging of the Spirit of God, he went into a Gentile home in the Roman garrison town of Caesarea. When he entered the house, he said, "You are well aware that it is against our law for a Jew to associate with a Gentile or to visit him. But God has shown me that I should not call any man impure or unclean" (Acts 10:28). God was working on Peter's heart to tear down a wall of prejudice which was older than his own lifetime.

Cornelius told Peter of a vision he had seen earlier in which an angel had instructed him to send for the apostle (Acts 10:30-33). Putting together all that had happened to him and to Cornelius, Peter drew this belated conclusion about the universality of the Christian religion: "I now realize how true it is that God does not show favoritism but accepts men from every nation who fear him and do what is right" (Acts 10:34b-35).

This incident paved the way for evangelistic work to begin in earnest among the non-Jews of the Roman Empire. The church was soon established at Antioch in Syria (Acts 11:19-26), and the first missionary tour by Paul was sponsored from there (Acts 13:1-3).

Even so, the issue was not yet resolved. When Paul returned from that first preaching tour, prejudiced Jews from Palestine came to Antioch and insisted that Paul (and thus the church at Antioch which had sent him out) had done wrong by accepting Gentiles into fellowship. They insisted that Gentiles would have to be saved in two steps: (1) Become Jews through circumcision and the other traditional rites of proselyting, and (2) be baptized into the spiritual body of Christ. "Some men came down from Judea to Antioch and were teaching the brothers: 'Unless you are circumcised, according to the custom taught by Moses, you cannot be saved' " (Acts 15:1).

The controversy created by Paul's work among the Gentiles resulted in a conference at Jerusalem which debated the matter in detail. By revelation from God, the people there were assured that Gentiles and Jews were to have equal access into the blessings of the gospel (Acts 15:12-29). The matter was formally resolved at the Jerusalem conference, but racism has continued to plague the progress of the church of God to the present day.

New Testament Teaching

The message of the New Testament is emphatic on the matter of prejudice and racism. *All races, colors, and languages are united in Christ.* "There is neither Jew nor Greek, slave nor free, male nor female, for you are all one in Christ Jesus" (Gal. 3:28). "Here there is no Greek or Jew, circumcised or uncircumcised, barbarian, Scythian, slave or free, but Christ is all and is in all" (Col. 3:11).

According to the Lord Jesus Christ, there are two great commandments on which hang all the Law and the Prophets: "Love the Lord your God with all your heart and with all your soul and with all your mind" and "Love your neighbor as yourself" (Matt. 22:37-40). It is this basic obligation of love to God and one's fellow human beings which destroys old prejudices and allows the functioning of the body of Christ as a united fellowship.

The apostle John picked up the theme of loving God and man in his first epistle. He wrote: "If we love each other, God lives in us and his love is made complete in us" (1 John 4:12b). Then, in the strongest possible language, he says: "If anyone says, 'I love God,' yet hates his brother, he is a liar. For anyone who does not love his brother, whom he has seen, cannot love God, whom he has not seen. And he has given us this command: Whoever loves God must also love his brother" (1 John 4:20-21).

As Richard Halverson has summed it up, the New Testament says this about Christianity and racism: "Godliness issues in mutual respect and love. No fact is more manifest in the Scriptures. Christian faith dissolves human prejudice. Faith that does not do so, whatever its profession, is not just sub-Christian; it is a contradiction."

To the church has been committed a ministry of reconciliation. Therefore we cannot be about the business — whether teen-ager or elder in the church — of perpetuating unhealthy attitudes toward other human beings who are created in the image of God. Laws and court decrees cannot destroy racism. Conversion, love, and true faith will.

Racism is a Moral Issue

It will not do to say that prejudice is a social issue and not a moral one. To be sure, racism shows itself in society. But that admission is not equivalent to saying that it is *merely* a social issue which is without ethical implications. One might as well try to argue that rape is a social issue and not a moral one.

Rape is a moral as well as social matter because it (1) involves an offense against another human being and (2) entails a violation of the Golden Rule.

First, it is an offense against a human being. Rape is an aggressive and hurtful assault against a person. It treats another person as a thing, an object of contempt. It refuses to recognize the sacredness of that person as a being in God's image and entitled to make free decisions about the use of her/his body.

Second, it clearly violates the basic ethical principle which governs human interaction. The Golden Rule requires that we treat others only as we would want them to treat us (Matt. 7:12). The sexual and personal violence which are involved in rape cannot be desired by a normal person and thus cannot be willed to others. For example, the rapist does not want to be a victim of his own crime or have his parents or children so abused.

*Racism is a moral issue precisely because of these same two factors.*First, racial prejudice involves **an offense against another human being.** According to the Bible, all men and women on planet Earth are descendants of Adam and Eve. The origin of different races and languages among humanity is explained in terms of the scattering of people from the Tower of Babel (cf. Gen. 11:1-9). So, whatever differences of skin color, language, or geographical homeland are relevant to people, we are every one in God's image and worthy of respect as *persons*. Racism is a painful aggression against people because of the accidental features of color, language, or national origin. To deny people their rights as human beings, to make fun of or to sneer at people because of their race, or to treat them as essentially inferior is to sin against them. It is to refuse to acknowledge their sacredness as persons in the image of God. It treats them as sub-humans or non-humans and subjects them to abuse.

Second, racism is certainly **a violation of the Golden Rule.** No normal human being wants to be denied his or her rights as a person. None of us wants to be mistreated because he is a Rebel or Yankee, Mexican-American or Amer-Asian, black or white. When one of us is snubbed or treated disrespectfully on the basis of such factors as these, outrage is the normal reaction. By the principle of the Golden Rule, then, I have no right to snub or mistreat someone who is different from me and the people with whom I am most comfortable. If I do so, I ought not be surprised at having generated resentment.

I happen to be white, male, and American. I have no apology to make for any of these accidental features of my being. Furthermore, I was morally incensed several years ago at the Iranian action of holding white American males as hostages — precisely and only because they were white American males. In fact, I had to fight back the very real temptation to have prejudiced feelings toward Iranians because of what was going on at the time. What I felt then in reaction to that situation must be something akin to what many other people — from male Greek slaves in the Roman Empire to female black Southerners in America — have had to deal with on an even larger scale. Even then the comparison is a poor one, for I did not suffer personal humiliation, deprivation of liberty, or abuse of my person.

An American Crisis

Except for the American Indian (who has also been the object of terrible racial prejudice and injustice), the Negro is this country's oldest ethnic minority. Anyone who denies that black people have been shamefully abused and oppressed in this society is either unaware of the facts of history or is deliberately closing his eyes to those facts.

Taken from their homes in Africa by force and brought to America under conditions now considered inhumane for animal shipment, black men and women were sold as slaves to American colonists and deprived of the dignity of personhood.

As agriculture assumed an increasingly prominent role in the life of colonial America, the exploitation of slave labor grew proportionately. By 1740 about 140,000 Negro slaves had been brought to this country. By the time of the Civil War, there were about four million slaves in the United States.

During the Civil War, Abraham Lincoln issued the Emancipation Proclamation on January 1, 1863, and declared the slaves to be free in those states which had broken away from the Union. Slavery was abolished in the nation at large when, on December 18, 1865, the Thirteenth Amendment to the Constitution became law.

As we know only too well, prejudice, intolerance, and racial hatred have not been eliminated by legislation from Washington. Even all the civil rights legislation of more recent years has not solved our problems.

When federal law began to bring about a redress of grievances for Afro-Americans in the 1960s, some black spokesmen began speaking of "Black Power." Black Power was to be a means of economic, social, and educational overthrow. If white people had to be hurt, deprived, and denied to gain such power, so much the worse for them. One wrong had generated another one.

Prejudice is wrong whether it is found among whites or blacks, Jews or Gentiles, Americans or Russians. The way to bring about healiing of old wounds is not through reversing roles between oppressor and oppressed, but by eliminating oppression altogether. Our common goal must be the creation of a society which is equitable for all its citizens — without regard to racial considerations.

The Cross as a Symbol

One of the most ungodly vestiges of racism to survive into modern times is the Ku Klux Klan. Founded about 1866 as a social group for Confederate veterans, it soon became an instrument of terror against blacks in the post-Civil War South. In 1871 Congress passed the Force Bills and thereby gave the president power to suppress the Klan as a conspiracy against the government. The original Ku Klux Klan soon disappeared.

In 1915 a new Klan was formed to spread its hatred toward Negroes, Jews, Catholics, and foreigners. Its membership topped two million in the 1920s but was formally dissolved in 1944. Following World War II and, especially, in connection with the Civil Rights movement of the 1960s, it blossomed again.

One of the many evils associated with the Ku Klux Klan is its use of the cross as one of its symbols. Its burning cross is one of the best-known trademarks in the world. I have seen only one in my life and cannot put into words the feelings it prompted.

The cross of Jesus Christ was designed to break down racial barriers, and its use as a symbol of racial hatred is a terrible irony. Commenting on the implications of the cross of Christ for Jew-Gentile relations, Paul wrote: "For he himself is our peace, who has made the two one and has destroyed the barrier, the dividing wall of hostility, by abolishing in his flesh the law with its commandments and regulations. His purpose was to create in himself one new man out of the two, thus making peace, and in this one body to reconcile both of them to God through the cross, by which he put to death their hostility. He came and preached peace to you who were far away and peace to those who were near. For through him we both have access to the Father by one Spirit" (Eph. 2:14-18).

To use the cross as a symbol for an organization which is dedicated to maintaining separation, perpetuating tensions, and arousing even more hatred among races is a monstrous offense against all the cross represents to the human race.

Anti-Semitism in America

Either racism or religious bigotry is hateful enough of itself. Anti-Semitism is an insidious blend of the two. Perhaps because of the merging of both racial and religious prejudice in one package, anti-Semitism continues to thrive — long after the segregation of blacks has officially ended and a quarter century after America elected a president who was Roman Catholic.

A national survey taken in 1986 polled a thousand white conservatives who wear the label "Christian." Ninety percent said they believe Christians should not have negative attitudes toward Jews as "killers of Christ." Sixty percent said "Jews can never be forgiven for what they did to Jesus until they accept him as the true savior." And one person expressed his view that God holds Jews responsible for Jesus' death "in the sense that they carried it out" and God has "dealt with them" since in historical events, including the millions of deaths in the Holocaust.

It is bad history, poor theology, and fundamental wrong-headedness to be thinking in those categories.

According to the New Testament, responsibility for the death of Christ lies with a broad class called "sinners" rather than with any sub-group such as Jew or Gentile, American or Russian, black or white. His death is traced to sin which began in Eden — before any racial distinctions were known. His death is linked to all races, cultures, ages, and individuals by virtue of moral and spiritual failure, not genetics. That certain Jews and Romans were present at his death — with Romans more directly responsible for it than Jews — is an accident of history.

According to the New Testament, Christianity is not a repudiation of Judaism but its fruition and fulfillment. Hatred toward Jews is nonsensical for people who embrace a Jewish peasant from Nazareth as divine. As a universal religion, the Christian faith teaches us to make no distinction among races.

According to the New Testament, God's kindness or sternness toward any particular individual is based on his or her personal faith, choices, and behavior in relation to the will of God. It is not based on race, color, language, nationality, economic status, or any similar factor.

Events like the Holocaust are caused by evil and/or insane men who set themselves against a God of love to wield power with hatred. I reject any God or theology which goes after innocent people generations removed from an event to extract vengeance. The decision to drop an atomic bomb on a war-waging nation in order to stop that war — even if many innocent people die from it — can be argued for with plausibility. The decision to drop that same bomb on that nation ten generations later and with its people living in peace would be morally reprehensible to any civilized person. Hitler and others like him brought on the Holocaust, not the God of the Christian Bible.

Do I want to evangelize Jews? Yes — along with Muslims, Hindus, Taoists, Buddhists, Sikhs, Eskimos, and some church deacons! As a Christian, I would like for all people to know about Jesus' claims and credentials for the sake of personal decision-making about him. I am not concerned to deny any person his ethnic heritage or to rescue him from some imagined curse on his race.

The immediate challenge to all of us is to live in respect, harmony, and love within a pluralistic society. And that cannot happen with Christians labeling Jews "Christ-killers." Such language can only be destructive to the "ministry of reconciliation" to which Christians have been called.

Conclusion

Christianity remains a unifying religion of reason and love. We must not lose sight of this important truth; we must never give way to irrationalism and hatred. *Christians must be unifiers and healers.*

Applying our four "Guidelines About Right and Wrong" is almost too easy on this issue. There are both explicit commands and general principles in Scripture which relate to racism. This chapter has surveyed many of those texts. Your influence for Christ and the church at school, at work, and in your neighborhood will be affected directly by your ability to love your neighbor as yourself and to practice the Golden Rule. Surely the godliest people in your sphere of acquaintances are people who know how to live in harmony with all people.

Second only to our obligation to love God, a Christian is under responsibility to love his or her neighbors — regardless of religion, color, national origin, or language. Following Christ rules out racist attitudes and behavior.

10 / Superstition, Astrology, and the Occult

The story of Christy Dennis appeared in the December 15, 1981, National Enquirer *under the headline: "HYP-NOTIZED HOUSEWIFE REVEALS: SPACE ALIENS TOOK ME TO 3 BIZARRE PLANETS." Mrs. Dennis, under hypnosis administered by Dr. R. Leo Sprinkle, revealed an abduction to an underground city on a distant planet. She met inhabitants eight to ten feet tall. She saw a violet sky, blue trees, and purple water. Houses were built underground to preserve the beauty of their world. Dr. Sprinkle, a counseling psychologist at the University of Wyoming and an investigator of UFO abductions, was quoted as saying, "This is one of the most remarkable cases I've ever come across." The* Enquirer *said the possibility that the story it carried was a hoax "has been ruled out not only through lie detection tests but through hypnotic regression."*

Early in 1983, Dr. Sprinkle received a letter from Mrs. Dennis. "Now is the time for me to reclaim my integrity and to establish myself in Truth," she wrote. "I am not a contactee. I have never had an extraterrestrial experience." She confessed that she had concocted her story to call attention to her views about problems on planet Earth. To Dr. Sprinkle's credit, he promptly released copies of Mrs. Dennis' confession and apologized for his unwitting role in the deception.

Recently I participated in a three-way conversation with a physician who is deeply into what has come to be known

97

as "New Age thinking," a phenomenon being popularized by Shirley MacLaine. As he explained a tragic diagnosis of fatal illness to a patient's wife, he used the term "spiritual strength" to her. Since she and I are Christians and interpreted that term as one relating to faith in God, she looked at him and asked, "Oh, are you a Christian?" The physician said, "No, I am not a Christian." Then, with a bit of a nervous smile on his face, he said, "But I call myself a believer." "You believe in God," the lady pressed, "but just don't go to church?" "My wife and I believe in our own divinity," he said. "I guess you could say that we worship ourselves — life, beauty, music, and anything which makes us feel good about our existence."

Many Dallas Cowboy fans cringe when they see their favorite team come on the field wearing blue jerseys. They believe the blue uniforms jinx their team. Some folks think breaking a mirror brings seven years of bad luck or that a black cat crossing their path means trouble. Many won't walk under ladders. Others carry a rabbit's foot or other good luck charm. Many hospitals, hotels, and other tall buildings don't have thirteenth floors.

A *superstition* is the belief that some action or circumstance which is not logically related to a series of events influences its outcome. Are superstitious ideas about black cats and blue football jerseys harmless? Or are there dangers involved?

A most ancient form of superstition involves signs of the zodiac, horoscopes, and fortune telling. *Astrology* claims to be able to forecast human events by observing and interpreting the heavenly bodies. It is founded on a belief in the *occult* (i.e., hidden, mysterious, supernatural) influence of the sun, moon, planets, and stars on human affairs. Great importance is attached to knowing precisely when and where a person was born.

An Ancient Phenomenon

The history of astrology can be traced back at least as far as the Babylonians of the second millennium before

Christ. It was already a well-developed practice among them by the time of Daniel (cf. Dan. 2:10-11). His ability to interpret the dreams of Nebuchadnezzar and to predict future events unfailingly stood him in sharp contrast with the astrologers and star-gazers of the Babylonians.

Some scholars believe the Tower of Babel incident (Gen. 11) had as its objective the building of a high platform for sun and moon worship. The pyramids of ancient Egypt and Mexico were built with astrological functions in mind. During the period of Greek supremacy in world history, the first horoscopes were developed.

Astrology was quite popular among the masses of the Roman Empire at the time of Christ and the apostles. Astrologers and soothsayers had a great following not only among the common people but also among the superstitious emperors of Rome. Both Tiberius and Nero are known to have relied heavily on astrologers for deciding affairs of state, and Augustus had a coin issued with his sign of the zodiac, Capricorn, imprinted on it.

The attitude God has asked his people to take toward everything connected with superstition, astrology, and the occult has remained consistent through the ages. He has warned against everything associated with them.

As the Israelites were being prepared for entry into Canaan, they were told: "When you enter the land the Lord your God is giving you, do not learn to imitate the detestable ways of the nations there. Let no one be found among you who sacrifices his son or daughter in the fire, who practices divination or sorcery, interprets omens, engages in witchcraft, or casts spells, or who is a medium or spiritist or who consults the dead. Anyone who does these things is detestable to the Lord" (Deut. 18:9-12a).

Centuries later the prophet Jeremiah reminded the people of Yahweh's attitude toward such things. He wrote: "Do not learn the ways of the nations or be terrified by signs in the sky, though the nations are terrified by them. For the customs of the peoples are worthless" (Jer. 10:2-3a; cf. 8:1-2).

The teaching of the New Testament is no less emphatic. On his first missionary journey, Paul had an encounter with a man named Bar-Jesus. The Greek text calls him a *magos,* a word translated "sorcerer" or "magician" in our English Bibles and which refers to one who is expert in astrology. The Spirit-given rebuke of the man is one of the sternest in all the Bible: "You are a child of the devil and an enemy of everything that is right! You are full of all kinds of deceit and trickery. Will you never stop perverting the right ways of the Lord?" (Acts 13:10). Simon of Samaria (Acts 8:9ff) was also involved in the practice of sorcery before his conversion to Christ. The burning of many valuable scrolls at Ephesus (Acts 19:19) seems to have been connected with the turning of people away from sorcery in connection with their conversion to Christ.

Another term for the practice of occult arts (Gk, *pharmakeia* = sorcery, witchcraft) is listed with the works of the flesh in Galatians 5:20, and those involved with such practices will be sentenced to eternal punishment, according to Revelation 21:8.

The occasional claim that Old and New Testament prophets were astrologers of centuries past is utterly without foundation. As Tony Sargent has written on this point: "In close contact with the living God, these men warned the people against the occult. Predictions they made from time to time came from their contact with the Lord who sovereignly disclosed his intentions to his friends. The claim that the wise men were astrologers is nonsense. They made no references to any conjunctions of the planets, horoscopes, or readings of the zodiac. Possibly they were Gentile converts familiar with the prophecy of Numbers 24:17. They depended not on charts, but on guidance from the Lord God (Matt. 2:12)."

As Christianity spread in the first-century world, astrology and other forms of occult superstition waned.

Renewed Interest in the Occult

One might expect the story of horoscopes, crystal balls, necromancy, and the like to end at this point. Yet in most eastern cultures, astrology has never been generally excluded from the public mentality. As the church went into a period of apostasy which reached its zenith in the Middle Ages, the hold of occult practices became very prominent again. Several medieval popes consulted astrologers regularly, and the gullible public went along with even more bizarre involvements in witchcraft and sorcery.

Even though we live in a "scientific age" and pride ourselves on being freed from the ignorance of past times, the rise of occult superstitions has been nothing short of frightening in the past few decades.

Jeane Dixon has made herself quite a name as a seer. "But hasn't she made some correct predictions?" someone asks. Yes. But her rate of success is no better than the guessing average of any informed person. For example, she predicted that Pope Paul would enjoy a year of good health, but he died in that same year; she said the Panama Canal treaties would be defeated in Congress, and they were approved; she told her readers that Marie Osmond would not marry in the foreseeable future, and two months later she did; she informed the world that Ted Kennedy would be elected President in 1980, but he wasn't. Lists of her failures are published only by those of us who keep tabs on her. Her editors and publishers report only the predictions that come true. The money continues to roll in from those who choose to believe in her.

Uri Geller earns hundreds of thousands of dollars from his displays of telepathy and psychokinesis — using the mind to control objects. He has bent spoons and keys on "The Tonight Show" without touching them. He is an impressive performer and commands big fees, although his feats have been duplicated by magicians who flatly say they are illusions and tricks.

Magician James Randi, for example, has duplicated the deeds of stage psychics and offered $10,000 to anyone who can demonstrate genuine "psychic powers" before a group of informed experts such as himself. The well-publicized offer has been standing for approximately 20 years. On occasion he has even surrendered a $10,000 cashier's check to an impartial jury to judge whether the claimed feat has been performed under the agreed-upon conditions. As of this writing, no true psychic has been discovered who could claim the money. If there were such persons with genuine psychic abilities, surely they would have welcomed the opportunity to claim the money, convince the skeptics, and educate us about such phenomena.

Americans in large numbers are paying out huge sums of money to participate in the secrets of "paranormal" experience. Portable astrological computers which cut to seconds the time needed to construct an astrological chart sell from $1,000 to $3,200. About 10,000 full-time astrologers practice in the United States, charging from $50 to $300 to advise their clients on important decisions; an estimated 175,000 are part-time practitioners who get smaller fees. At no time in history have there been more astrologers than there are today.

Millions of dollars are spent annually on the books, magazines, and other paraphernalia of the occult. Practically every major newspaper in the country carries daily horoscopes.

Gallup polls indicate that the number of Americans who take astrology seriously has doubled from the estimated total of the early 1970s — now totaling around 32 million. Over one-fifth of all the persons interviewed in one poll said they believe in astrology to one degree or another, and nearly one-fourth said they read an astrology column regularly. The same poll revealed that 77 percent of all respondents knew their "sign," and 90 percent of those under 30 knew theirs.

A Gallup Youth Survey done about the same time as the poll mentioned above showed that a remarkable 40 percent of teen-agers believe in astrology. Teen-age girls are especially likely to pay serious attention to it.

One scientist, an astronomer, has put his finger on one of the primary reasons for the new popularity of such phenomena: "In these uncertain times, many long for the comfort of having guidance in making decisions. They would like to believe in a destiny predetermined by astral forces beyond their control."

From a Christian point of view, I would go further to say that it is a testimony to the spiritual barrenness of our time. Far from being a harmless fad, it is a *revival of paganism* and a retreat from both reason and revelation.

New Age Thinking

Judging from bookshelves, newspapers, and television, one of the most popular turns in America's penchant for new things takes the form of what is variously called the New Age Movement, cosmic consciousness, self-realization, or spiritualism. And it is too glib to dismiss the people caught up in it as nuts, wierdos, and flakes. While some of the people involved may be charlatans, many are intense and sincere.

Celebrities such as Tina Turner, John Denver, and Carly Simon not only follow this movement but urge it upon others. But there is no better salesperson for this new movement than Shirley MacLaine.

Shirley MacLaine is an outstanding actress and articulate spokesperson. She has written two books which chronicle her conversion to New Age mysticism. In *Out on a Limb* and *Dancing in the Light,* she describes her belief in and alleged experiences with reincarnation, UFOs, extraterrestrials (especially one she calls "Mayan"), communication with astral-plane spirits through seances, out-of-body experiences, and the like. She went on a national tour promoting New Age thinking. And ABC aired a movie-version of her beliefs in the spring of 1987 which was watched by millions.

While I am grateful for anyone's determination to seek after the sacred, I am frightened by this recent trend toward synthesizing Eastern thought and Christianity. It is a wrong turn along the way to genuine spirituality. It is antithetical to New Testament Christianity and has already confused the minds of thousands of impressionable people. After all, our generation is not known for critical thinking. From politicians to appliances to religion, a celebrity endorsement and glitzy packaging go further in gaining acceptance than product merit.

Ms. MacLaine's primary themes reduce to the following: (1) all of us are divine and can attain identity with the One, (2) each of us has lived before and will live again by virtue of reincarnation, (3) each of us is working to perfection through reincarnation by facing and overcoming the imperfections of previous lives [i.e., the doctrine of "karma"], (4) there are as many realities/truths as there are people because each person creates his own reality/truth, and (5) there is no such thing as death.

To some people these themes are far-fetched and bizarre. So why bother taking note of Ms. MacLaine and New Age thinking? Doesn't it just call attention to something most people would ignore? Might calling attention to it serve the purpose of publicizing her message? Perhaps. But there seem to be compelling reasons for thinking that something needs to be said about this movement.

First, thousands of people have been confused by her books, speeches, and television publicity. I would like to help just a few of those people to think through her claims from a Christian perspective.

Second, Ms. MacLaine has quoted Jesus and the Bible liberally in support of her themes. People need to know that her use of Scripture is wrong-headed and deceptive. The Bible stands unalterably against the sorts of phenomena she alleges and encourages others to seek as "Spiritual."

Third, something which is as diametrically opposed to the Christian faith as the New Age theory cannot be allowed to go unchallenged by people who are committed to Jesus. Against the view that all religious views are right and all are wrong, Christianity makes exclusive claims for itself. Jesus Christ claims to be *the* way to God (cf. John 14:6). And a system of thought so antithetical to Christianity as Ms. MacLaine's surely comes under the rubric of this statement from Paul: "Have nothing to do with the fruitless deeds of darkness, but rather expose them"(Eph. 5:11).

The essence of "cosmic consciousness" or New Age thinking is its thesis of *self-realization*. In other words, its devotees worship at the shrine of self. It is an enthronement of pride and egoism. Self-realization translates into self-worship of the sort mentioned in the second case study at the beginning of this chapter.

Shirley MacLaine puts it this way: "The knowingness of our divinity is the highest intelligence. And to *be* what we already know is the free will. Free will is simply the enactment of the realization you are God, a realization that you are divine: free will is making everything accessible to you."

There is nothing compatible with a thesis such as this and the Bible. It is man's exaltation of himself, from Eden to Calvary, which has been the bane of his existence. Pride is the source of man's rejection of God's authority over human life and the basis for disobedience to every command that has ever been given to the race.

Contrary to the notion that we need more *self*-awareness, *self*-consciousness, and *self*-realization, the truth is that we need far less attention with self and more concern for others. One almost gets the feeling that this verse was put into the Bible for people who are preoccupied with the task of finding themselves: "Whoever finds his life will lose it, and whoever loses his life for my sake will find it" (Matt. 10:39). The New Age movement rejects the claim of any neighbor which infringes on personal interests, and that is just another form of unvarnished selfishness — the root of all our miseries in this world.

As LaGard Smith puts it: "In showing us how to be truly fulfilled, Jesus taught that we need to lay down our lives for others — not to be more self-assertive. In order to fully live, we must die to our selves. Self-direction must be turned into self-denial. To find ourselves, we must lose ourselves. True self-actualization comes through giving up self to the lordship of Christ. When we are committed to loving and serving Christ and others, we will not be consumed by the void that eats at us when we are wrapped up in ourselves." [Note: Dr. Smith has written a careful and thorough study of Shirley MacLaine's theories about life. His *Out on a Broken Limb* (Eugene, OR: Harvest House Publishers, 1986) is an excellent resource book to anyone confused by New Age thinking.]

The two basic fallacies of this syncretized form of Eastern religion have to do with its attitude toward God and self.

First, New Age thought has no place for the God of the Bible. Self reigns supreme, and no God external to one's own self needs to be sought.

This anti-Christian system is a form of philosophical monism. It holds that all of reality is continuous and without boundaries: "all is one." This means that there are not many selves but one Self, the One. All is one; all is good; all is God. It is *pantheism* revived for moderns.

From a biblical point of view, God is a personal Being who is other than his creation and who created human beings in diversity. Things, events, animals, and persons are not a continous whole but a genuine plurality. We are in the image of God (Gen.1:26-27), but we are not God. It is by Christ's creative power that "all things hold together" within the universe (Col. 1:17), but it is not true that all things are one. God's will is to reconcile sinners to himself (2 Cor. 5:17-21), but we are not divine and do not share his essence. As a matter of fact, Scripture both affirms God's distinctiveness from his created world and identifies as paganism the confusion of the two in this statement: "They exchanged the truth of God for a lie, and worshiped and served created things rather than the Creator — who is forever praised" (Rom. 1:25).

Second, just as surely as this trendy movement rejects the God of Scripture, it also strikes at the very thing it is supposed to affirm — self-worth.

The worth of a single life which is just one more installment in a potentially endless series of reincarnations becomes nil. Bad karma from this life will be balanced with a punishment in the next one; good karma this time will generate a benefit of some sort. As Ms. MacLaine puts it, reincarnation "is like show business. You just keep doing it until you get it right." But there is no reason to take any one of these serial lives too seriously, for everything will resolve itself somewhere down the line. On the New Age pattern of things, some future and unforeseen form of your transmigrational self will achieve self-redemption.

Reincarnation cannot be squared with biblical truth. The writer of Hebrews affirms that "man is destined to die once, and after that to face judgment" (Heb. 9:27). The life you are living now is meaningful to the ultimate degree. Your eternal welfare is being determined by the choices, moral commitments, and spiritual values you are living now. To someone who is living in rebellion against God and unprepared to face judgment, the notion of multiple life-death-rebirth cycles is a handy source of escape from responsibility. The Christian religion is the only one which will meet the real needs of people.

First, people need a sense of *genuine self-worth.* New Age spokesmen strike a responsive chord when they raise this issue with our contemporaries. But, as I have shown already, their system fails to provide what it promises on this point. The tenets of reincarnation and karma undermine self-esteem and make one's life less meaningful rather than more meaningful.

The Bible teaches that God has created you in his own image. When Jesus went to the cross, it was because of a love for you which is intense and personal. When you come to God through Christ, you are adopted into God's family, made a joint-heir with Christ, and given a purpose for your life. "And God raised us up with Christ and seated us with him in the heavenly realms in Christ Jesus, in order that in the coming ages he might show the incomparable riches of his grace, expressed in his kindness to us in Christ Jesus" (Eph. 2:6-7; cf. 1:11-14).

Second, everyone needs a sense *personal freedom.* The Christian religion is often perceived to be an enslaving thing. Indeed, in both Catholic and Protestant traditions, ecclesiastical power can be shown to achieve that very end. In our culture, however, personal freedom and decision-making are praised. The notion of having a church and its creed or a priest-pastor to do your thinking for you doesn't sit well with most of us.

Again, however, the Christianity of the Bible is different. Jesus talked about the truth setting men free rather than ens-laving them (John 8:32). And Paul wrote: "It is for freedom that Christ has set us free. Stand firm, then, and do not let yourselves be burdened again by a yoke of slavery" (Gal. 5:1). The misuse of religion to fetter thought and take away free-dom has driven away many sensitive souls.

Third, we need a positive hope of *transcending earthly exis-tence,* an existence which is sometimes painful. From ancient Greece through Eastern religion to cosmic consciousness, the hope of transcendance has been held out in the form of astral bodies and freeing the spirit from its prison of flesh.

Christianity offers something better. In the here and now, we know we have the compassion of Jesus in our sufferings; he experienced human life and can understand our frailties (Heb. 2:18). More than that, we have the promise that our experiences are not karmic balance from a previous life, but are events which God will use to change us into his likeness. "And we, who with unveiled faces all reflect the Lord's glory, are being transformed into his likeness with ever-increasing glory, which comes from the Lord, who is the Spirit" (2 Cor. 3:18). Then, at the end of life on earth, both spirit and body will be redeemed for eternity in heaven (1 Cor. 15:50-57).

Conclusion

The things discussed in this chapter taken collectively constitute a form of "powerful delusion" which human beings are allowed to believe if they prefer error to truth, wickedness to righteousness (cf. 2 Thess. 2:10-12).

There is not a single case on record where individuals have been able to demonstrate ESP, telepathic communication, psychokinesis, reincarnation, contact with extraterrestrials, or Satanic "powers" to the satisfaction of independent researchers. Even John Beloff, past president of the Parapsychological Association, admits as much: "No experiment of the paranormal has been consistently repeated by other investigators in other laboratories." Sensitive psychics cannot perform under pressure, they say; paranormal energies are too easily disrupted by the presence of doubters, they claim. Jesus, the apostles, and other men with genuine supernatural powers could exhibit them as needed for right purposes and were not dependent on the credulity of those who were watching. This is a stark contrast between the false and the true.

Our understanding of life and its real meaning is not found in the stars or from some Eastern guru, but in the Bible. *All supernatural knowledge of the human condition and all legitimate direction for the conduct of human lives comes from God through his Word.* Neither Satan, demons, nor the spirits of departed people can speak to human beings today (cf. Luke 16:27ff). God does not speak through omens, fortune tellers, ESP, dreams, or cards; he speaks to us only through the written Word (2 Pet. 1:3; 2 Tim. 3:16-17).

It is not only foolish but *sinful* to look elsewhere than to God for the guidance you need for your life.

11 / A Bridle For Your Tongue

The British tabloid press dubbed him "Mac the Mouth."
His tantrums, screaming at officials, and profanity on court
have been notorious in major tennis tournaments around
the world. Before Wimbledon 1984, officials of the All
England Club served notice that it would be tolerated no
more. The "gentlemanly sport" of tennis in England would
not be held hostage to John McEnroe any longer. There
would be warning, forfeiture, and then dismissal from the
tournament. Whether from quick maturity or in response
to the strict warnings, John McEnroe took to the courts,
behaved as a gentleman, and curbed his infamous tongue.
He turned in one of the most brilliant championship games
ever at Wimbledon against Jimmy Connors on July 8,
defeating him 6-1, 6-1, 6-2. The first American to win back-
to-back Wimbledon championships since 1938 was, to
quote the British Daily Express, *"on model behavior dur-*
ing the championship."

The story is told of an Egyptian ruler named Amasis
who sent a sacrificial animal to the residence of a respected
sage. His request of the wise man was that he send back
the best part and the worst part to his sovereign. To the
surprise of the monarch, not two parts but one was
returned to him. The tongue was sent back as that which
is both best and worst in any living thing.

The Bible teaches that the name of God must be treated
with special reverence. "You shall not misuse the name of

the Lord your God, for the Lord will not hold anyone guiltless who misuses his name" (Ex. 20:7). "He provided redemption for his people; he ordained his covenant forever — holy and awesome is his name" (Psa. 111:9). Since one's name stands for his character and person, God's name must be held in reverence and treated with honor.

One behavior trait which separates believers from unbelievers is the wrong use of God's name by the latter. Many conscientious Christians work hard not only to keep these obvious wrong uses of the holy name out of their vocabularies but also such slang versions of God's name as are commonly used in words such as "gosh," "Goldarn it," and "gee whiz."

Oaths, curses, slurs, and obscene gestures have been a part of society since the beginning of history. Scholars have found curses carved in Egyptian hieroglyphics and in almost every culture since. Harry Truman's speech even became something of a campaign issue, and the phrase "expletive deleted" became familiar with the release of Richard Nixon's White House tapes.

We've come a long way since Clark Gable had to get a special waiver from the industry's censorship code to use a four-letter word in *Gone With the Wind.* What was unthinkable in public a few decades ago can now be heard with regularity in the halls of elementary schools and on television. The slightly vulgar to the patently obscene can be overheard in casual conversations. The age, sex, race, or social status of the participants seem not to alter the language considerably.

Obscene speech is now out in public earshot, and it may be impossible to push it back behind closed doors. Young people who are attempting to live under the Lordship of Jesus Christ will need to give serious thought to the language they will use.

Christian Responsibility

One of the things God-fearing people are to eliminate from our lives is "filthy language from your lips" (Col. 3:8). Paul wrote: "Do not let any unwholesome talk come out of your mouths, but only what is helpful for building others up according to their needs, that it may benefit those who listen" (Eph. 4:29).

Profanity, off-color stories, racial slurs, lying, swearing, and similar wrong uses of the tongue have no place in the life of a young man or woman who wears the name of Christ. The Word of God teaches that we are not through with our words once they have been spoken. Jesus warned: "But I tell you that men will have to give account on the day of judgment for every careless word they have spoken. For by your words you will be acquitted, and by your words you will be condemned" (Matt. 12:36-37).

In the immediate context of the verses just cited, Jesus was teaching that what comes from the mouth reveals the condition of the speaker's heart. "For out of the overflow of the heart the mouth speaks," he said (Matt. 12:34b). What is in the heart that produces profanity?

Some experts think that the remarkable spread of profanity reflects the "me-generation" mentality which came to the forefront in the 1970s. An alienated, self-centered, and sometimes antisocial culture began to use language which expressed contempt for traditional institutions which had held our society together.

Dr. Thomas Cottle, a Harvard lecturer in psychiatry, attributes much of the phenomenon to anger and aggressiveness in people. "People are finding their lives phony, unsatisfying, and they are angry," he says. "When you have an attempt to normalize or make neutral words that are traditionally profane, you are looking at a very major change in American culture — more important than the fact more people are using swearwords."

Many psychologists and sociologists have observed that cursing and obscene language reflect personal insecurity. Sometimes the language is used merely to call attention to oneself. At other times, it is an effort to be accepted, "to be one of the guys."

Shock and bewilderment are sometimes expressed with a profane use of the divine name. Someone receives bad news and cries, "Oh, my God!" At the scene of an accident or personal injury, one arrives and says, "Christ, what happened here!" Whatever else may be appropriate to say in these situations, to use the name of God as an exclamation is *not* appropriate.

Sometimes it is something no more complex than a temper out of bounds which lies behind cursing and obscene speech. The offended person utters a vile prayer that asks God to damn someone who is made in the divine image and who is a neighbor to the one speaking.

Christian responsibility calls for a much more judicious use of the divine name. Worship, prayer, confession of faith in Jesus — these are proper uses of God's name.

A Study of James 3

The best-known and perhaps most important biblical text giving counsel about the tongue is the third chapter of James. The first verse of the chapter is a specific warning to Christian teachers about the control of their tongues. The remainder of the chapter, however, is not limited in application to public teachers of the gospel. It is a general warning to all believers about the need to bridle the tongue.

How much of an indicator is the tongue to the whole of one's character? James writes: "We all stumble in many ways. If anyone is never at fault in what he says, he is a perfect man, able to keep his whole body in check" (v.2). From this verse and what follows, he appears to be saying that most any other part of the body can be put under control more easily and effectively than the tongue. It is unruly, rebellious, and untamable.

To emphasize how powerful the tongue is, several impressive analogies are used in the chapter. It is like a spirited, violent horse that needs reining in by bit and bridle (v.3). A tongue out of control is like a ship loose from its moorings; it threatens to crash its owner's entire life on the rocks. Thus the pilot must have his hand on the wheel constantly (v.4).

Of all the figures used in James 3, none is more graphic than the one involving the fire and the forest: "Likewise the tongue is a small part of the body, but it makes great boasts. Consider what a great forest is set on fire by a small spark. The tongue also is a fire, a world of evil among the parts of the body. It corrupts the whole person, sets the whole course of his life on fire, and is itself set on fire by hell" (vs.5-6).

Fire can warm weary travelers and cook a family's food; on the other hand, uncontrolled fire can destroy both property and lives. Fire itself is neither good nor bad. Its help or harm depends on its use in particular settings. So it is with the tongue. The gift of speech is neither good nor evil. All depends on the use we make of it. The tongue can inspire, teach, and praise; it can also defeat, blaspheme, and discourage.

Churches divide, families break up, and friendships are destroyed by the spark struck from an angry word. So James says that an out-of-control tongue can "set the whole course of [a person's] life on fire." Such a tongue burns "with a flame fed by hell" (Williams).

James sounds pessimistic when he points out that we can tame all the creatures of nature (v.7), but "no man can tame the tongue" (v.8a). No one can ever have his tongue so completely under control that he or she can neglect it, remove the bridle, and allow it to run free. It always bears watching. "It is a restless evil, full of deadly poison" (v.8b).

The ultimate of inconsistencies in the life of a child of God is to allow the tongue to be used for the contradictory purposes of praising God on the one hand and cursing men on the other (v.9). "Out of the same mouth come praise and cursing. My brothers, this should not be" (v.10). It is as if James had attended a worship service with some of these brothers on Sunday morning, sung "Praise God From Whom All Blessings Flow" with them, and then heard them get angry and spew verbal venom on Monday. God expects us to be consistent in character with our words (vs.11-12).

Things to Guard Against

Besides **profanity** and **cursing**, there are other wrong uses of the tongue which young Christians ought to avoid.

Are you ever tempted to **gossip** about someone? It is amazing how false reports can get started. Some religious papers reported a while back about hearing company executives for some major corporations making comments about devil worship on "20/20" and "Phil Donahue" — though such conversations never took place. More recently the rumor circulated for three weeks that a youngster died from snapping his neck while doing a breakdancing scene for a soft-drink commercial. Newspapers and TV were used to quash the rumor.

Rumors get started in your school about someone doing drugs, being pregnant, or being drunk last weekend. Don't become part of the process. Don't encourage it by lending your ear to someone else who has a tale to tell. If someone blurts out something unflattering about another person without your request, suggest the biblical solution of having that person go with you to the one about whom it has been told (cf. Matt. 18:15-18).

Have you ever been tempted to **lie** to cover your tracks? Don't. Lying is one of the things the Lord hates (Prov. 6:17b). You don't want to be part of something which is so contradictory to the nature of the God in whom you believe. He is a God of Truth (John 3:33), and you reflect dishonor to him by deceitful behavior and lying words.

Then there are always the **dirty jokes** and **off-color stories** which circulate on campus. It isn't enough that you refuse to tell the stories which are most vulgar. Do you listen? Laugh? Encourage others to tell them? It isn't difficult to see that the person who delights in such stories is having a problem with purity of heart.

Instead of filling your conversation with suggestive tales, why not try the biblical pattern of healthy speech? "Let your conversation be always full of grace, seasoned with salt, so that you may know how to answer everyone" (Col. 4:6).

If you are talking with an individual or group and the direction of the conversation turns the wrong way, try getting it back on course. Ask about school activities. Ask what plans for the weekend are being made. Ask about plans for summer work or vacations. If the direction of talk can't be put back on a healthy track, just excuse yourself and leave.

Conclusion

Your speech and your reaction to the language others use around you is an index to your total character. Thus it is an important thing to apply the "Guidelines" we have been using throughout this volume to the matter of daily conversation.

First, what are the specific commands and prohibitions of the Word of God which apply here? Several of them have been listed and studied in this chapter. On the forbidden list are profanity, cursing, gossip, off-color stories, and lying. On the list of required things are truthfulness, reverent use of God's name in praise, speaking the gospel, and encouraging people in things that are right.

Second, what are the general principles which relate to speech? Ephesians 4:29 seems to be the best summary verse to use in answer to this question. We should learn to use speech that "builds others up" and gives "benefit to those who listen."

Third, are there implications for your Christian influence in the speech you use? No one is going to be anxious to hear about the precious name of Jesus from a mouth that has been used to spread filth, lies, or gossip.

Fourth, what of the best people you know? Do they use God's name to curse and take oaths? Do they tell lies and dirty jokes? The very thought is absurd.

The purpose of bridling either a horse or a tongue is not to take away its spirit and energy but to channel that power constructively. Your tongue will never be so thoroughly tamed that you can become careless with it. Place a bridle there now, keep the reins in hand, and discipline that unruly member of your body to the glory of the Lord Jesus.

12 / Blushing Is a Healthy Sign

Lisa was 14 when it happened. Security personnel in a mall caught her trying her hand at shoplifting. She tried to hide a blouse under her heavy winter coat and take it from the store, but she didn't get away with it. Her parents were called to the mall. Lisa was embarrassed beyond words, and her mom and dad were frightened for her. They not only punished her for what she had done but got her help by taking her to a psychologist. It has been over three years now. She's doing fine. Getting caught that day has turned out to be the best thing that could have happened to her.

Sixteen-year-old Kelly was caught shoplifting in the same store on the same day. She had told Lisa how easy it would be, and they went in and out of the store together. Her parents came, too, but things haven't turned out so well. Kelly lied and said she had forgotten having the bracelet on. She accused the guards of "laying a trap" for her. Her parents took her side and threatened to sue the mall. The past three years have been filled with increasingly serious incidents for Kelly. She's headed for really big trouble.

It is one thing to do something wrong; it is something else again to be proud (or at least, unashamed) of having done it. The former is bad; the latter is far worse.

That an individual is ashamed of having done something wrong means that he is still sensitive to spiritual things, that he can repent, that he can be forgiven. His inability to feel shame means that repentance is yet beyond him and that he cannot be forgiven.

119

Paul taught that "godly sorrow brings repentance that leads to salvation and brings no regret" (2 Cor. 7:10). David wrote: "The Lord is close to the brokenhearted and saves those who are crushed in spirit" (Psa. 34:18). Sin is no little thing, and it cannot be taken lightly. When a person who loves God realizes that he has broken the divine will through transgression, he will grieve. Realizing that he has broken God's heart as well as his law, his own heart will crumble and genuine repentance will result.

Right conduct before God begins with an attitude of heart. It has its roots in a God-oriented mind which is set on things above (Col. 3:2) and is therefore shocked and repulsed by evil (Rom. 12:9b).

This book cannot look at every topic of importance to the ethical behavior of a young Christian. Besides the specific items already treated, it would be worthwhile to look at other things such as gambling, modesty, and morality on the highway. In this chapter, however, I want to explore the more fundamental matter of spiritual sensitivity with you. If you will keep a tender conscience and learn to use the "Guidelines" we've been appealing to throughout this volume, you will do well in making all your moral decisions.

To test your heart as to its spiritual sensitivity, give honest answers to these questions: Do you feel at odds with society at large with its low values, or are you comfortable living by the same standards? Do reports of murder, rape, and scandal shock you, or are you so hardened to them that you hardly take notice anymore? Would you blush or otherwise show embarrassment if someone around you used the name of God in a profane manner, or would you be unaffected by it? And what about your own sins? Do you feel shame and remorse when you do wrong, or do you tell yourself that everybody you know does things a lot worse? Just what does it take to stir your conscience?

The Time of Jeremiah

About 600 years before the birth of Christ, Jeremiah was called of God to prophesy to the people of Judah in their darkest hour. Apostasy and moral degeneration had so weakened the nation that it was soon to be overrun by the Babylonians.

Prior to the terrible devastation of their country in 586 B.C., Jeremiah warned them of God's displeasure and called them to repent of their wicked ways. His tender pleadings and bitter tears for Jerusalem made him an outstanding type of Christ (Matt. 16:14; cf. Luke 19:41).

Jeremiah was unsuccessful in his efforts to get the people to turn back to God. Both stern warning and tender pleading fell on deaf ears. The inhabitants of Judah were too far gone for his message to reach them and produce repentance. The fault was not the prophet's, for he did all that was possible to accomplish his divinely appointed mission. The people of Judah fell because of their inability to feel shame for sin.

For example, God sent a drought throughout Judah to try to bring the people to their senses, but the nation was as brazen as a harlot and remained unmoved. "Therefore the showers have been withheld, and no spring rains have fallen. Yet you have the brazen look of a prostitute; you refuse to blush with shame" (Jer. 3:3). Later the prophet spoke of the sins which were bringing destruction on Jerusalem and lamented, "Are they ashamed of their loathsome conduct? No, they have no shame at all; they do not even know how to blush" (Jer. 6:15a). The very same words are repeated later: "Are they ashamed of their loathsome conduct? No, they have no shame at all; they do not even know how to blush" (Jer. 8:12a).

It was the judgment of God that these people were to be destroyed because their hearts were so hard and insensitive. They could not be ashamed of their sin. They had lost the ability to blush.

The sin described in these passages from Jeremiah is the same one which the Lord Jesus called "blasphemy against the Spirit" and labelled an "eternal sin" (Matt. 12:31-32; Mark 3:28-30). The sin which *cannot be forgiven* is not a specific act such as murder or fornication; it is a condition of heart which renders repentance hopeless and persistence in sin certain.

The apostle John wrote of the same sin and warned Christians of "a sin unto death" concerning which it was useless to pray for forgiveness (1 John 5:16). Since the same apostle assured his readers that God forgives any sin a Christian confesses (1 John 1:9), there can be no doubt that the sin heaven will not forgive is any sin for which one feels no shame and which his proud heart will not confess.

The verb *blush* means "to become red in the face especially from shame, modesty, or confusion; to feel shame or embarrassment." Without the feeling of shame and embarrassment over our transgressions of the will of God, there can be neither repentance nor forgiveness.

A Shameless World

The inability of the people of Judah to blush when confronted with their sins forces us to think of the situation in our world today. A large element of our society seems to be utterly without shame. The grossest of immoralities are paraded without any attempt to hide them. The attitude of the public generally appears to be that nothing is shocking anymore. Our world is "cool" and cynical when God would have us rage with indignation and hide our faces in shame.

According to an Associated Press report a while back, one of the major airlines was offering "a new service for passengers — printed cards telling how and where to meet prostitutes in New York, London, Paris, Rome, and Amsterdam." The same press service released a report about a church in Illinois which had conducted "nude therapy sessions" involving about 30 men and women; the minister said his district superintendent gave "his full support" to the program.

Actor Tony Curtis has boasted of "better parts" in today's movies because of the present philosophy of film-making. "They don't adhere to Christian morality any more. Now there are no more taboos," he said. Films without taboos play in theaters in every city of any size in America. Books and magazines compete for sales with stories of incest, rape, and pedophilia.

A society cannot tolerate this sort of shamelessness in its

public life without being affected in its corporate character and individual lives. Indeed, the proof is all around us.

Scandal among high government officials has brought about a situation where our national leaders are generally distrusted both at home and abroad. Laws prohibiting public drunkenness have been repealed in over half the 50 states, and several have now eliminated criminal penalties for possessing marijuana. Maine has eliminated prison terms for prostitution; several counties in Nevada have legalized it. Gambling is now sponsored by several of the 50 states, with at least 19 operating some form of lottery and 32 permitting some form of pari-mutuel betting.

There is no longer any serious stigma attached to divorce, and living together without the benefit of a marriage ceremony is commonplace. Out-of-wedlock births once meant that a girl would leave town to have her child and give the baby up for adoption; today it is permissible to stay at home, act as if nothing improper has happened, have the child, and celebrate its birth as if something to be proud of had taken place. Is our society simply beyond shame?

In the context of such shamelessness, Christians have not been uninfluenced. Members of the body of Christ once had a uniform attitude against drinking alcoholic beverages, but it is not too uncommon to hear social drinking defended now. The sexually explicit movements of many modern dances embarrass spiritually minded people, yet some teenagers insist on participating in them. No one with a pure heart can appear in the state of undress common to public beaches and pools without feeling ill at ease and being embarrassed by the presence of the equally immodest opposite sex. Dating couples go to movies which contain vulgar language, near or total nudity, and other scenes which should embarrass them too much to permit them to sit through them. Then, on the way back from the movie, the same couple drives to a secluded parking spot. "But all we do is talk," protests someone. Maybe so, but you should have too much self-respect and concern for a good reputation to be "parking" on a date. Have we lost our ability to blush?

Shamelessness: A Work of the Flesh

In Galatians 5:19-21, Paul lists several things which are called "works of the flesh." The third item in this catalog of unholy things is "lasciviousness" (KJV, ASV), "licentiousness" (RSV), or "debauchery" (NIV). Greek lexicons agree that the word in the original text *aselgeia* calls attention to a lifestyle which has thrown restraint to the wind and shows no regard for decency or self-respect. In an excellent little book entitled *Flesh and Spirit,* William Barclay observes that the word

> indicates a love of sin so reckless and audacious that a man has ceased to care what God or man thinks of his actions. ... As Lightfoot sees it, the essence of *aselgeia* is that it has come to such a stage of sinning that it makes no attempt whatever to hide or cloak its sin; it is sin lost to shame....
>
> It is completely indifferent to public opinion and to public decency. A man may well begin to do a wrong thing in secret; at the beginning his one aim and desire may be to hide it from the eyes of men. He may love the wrong thing, and he may even be mastered by it, but he is still ashamed of it. But it is perfectly possible for him to come to a state when he does openly and blatantly that which he did secretly and in concealment. He may come to a stage of sin when he is so lost to shame that he no longer cares what others see, and what they may say, or what they may think. The terrible thing about *aselgeia* is that it is the act of a character which has lost that which ought to be its greatest defence — its self-respect, and its sense of shame.

It begins with any sinful act, whether great or small. The individual who has done something that he knows to be wrong then gets a warning signal from his conscience. That warning signal is something like pain in our physical bodies. It says that something irregular has occurred, that some adjustment needs to be made, that corrective action is called for. One responds to his conscience by either feeling ashamed

124

and moving to set the matter straight or by fighting back and ignoring the warning he is receiving.

If he chooses to fight his conscience and defend himself in something where he knows he has been wrong, something terrible starts to happen. He begins to "be hardened by sin's deceitfulness" (Heb. 3:13b). His self-respect goes and then his reputation. He now feels shut up to a life which matters to nobody. With all concern now gone about how his life is viewed, he lives in open and flagrant sin. Sometimes it appears that he deliberately seeks to flaunt his immoralities and to hurt anyone who would dare to care enough to try to help him.

Safeguards For Our Hearts

On the assumption that Christian young people do not want to lose their spiritual sensitivity by being molded into the image of the sinful world surrounding us or by taking the wrong attitude toward their own sins, here are three suggestions for protecting your heart which will help you.

First, **stay close to the Word of God.** Do not let a single day go by without spending time in the serious reading of Scripture. Read carefully, reflectively, and expectantly. Memorize key verses or sentences from what you read. One cannot be filling his or her heart with the Word daily without coming to see sin for what it really is.

The closer you stay to the Bible and the more you allow your thinking to be molded by it, the more you will come to hate sin, be repulsed by sin, and be embarrassed by sin. David wrote: "Because I consider all your precepts right, I hate every wrong path" (Psa. 119:128).

Second, **pay attention to your conscience.** Conscience is an internal monitor of one's behavior which gives a sense of assurance to the person who is doing what he has been taught to be right and a sense of uneasiness to the person who is violating the standard he has been taught. Yes, conscience is related to the things one has been taught and thus cannot be an altogether safe guide. It must be educated by Scripture and make its judgments on the basis of that absolute and true standard.

But in the case of a Christian who has been instructed in the Word of God and who daily stays close to it in his or her devotional life, conscience must be listened to. When you are getting too close to something that can hurt you, your conscience protests. When you are asked to participate in something that would damage your spirituality, conscience will warn you to stay away. If you violate the will of God you have been learning, conscience will prod you back toward the right with a sense of guilt.

Lest you lose your sensitivity to goodness, a young person living under the Lordship of Jesus must not ignore the guidance of conscience. Only by heeding this call can you keep your conscience clear before God and man (cf. Acts 24:16).

Third, if sin is weighing on your conscience now, confess it at once and seek **divine forgiveness.** Unrepented sin in the heart is like a hot coal in one's hands; it must be gotten rid of quickly, or it will burn and sear. So do not let it stay there another moment. Be ashamed. *Blush.* Let the remorse of your soul be genuine and lead you to repentance.

David described the torment of a guilty conscience this way: "My guilt has overwhelmed me like a burden too heavy to bear" (Psa. 38:4). Fighting the burden of a guilty conscience hardens the heart. Allowing conscience to stimulate repentance and change in one's life heals a broken relationship with God.

Conclusion

The attitude God would have all people of all ages to have toward their personal sins is the one demonstrated by David in his penitential prayer of Psalm 51. He had schemed, plotted, and sinned with Bathsheba. Then he tried to cover his deed and got into deeper trouble than ever (2 Sam. 11). Then came Nathan the prophet with the rebuke of the Word of God, and his heart melted (2 Sam. 12). He was ashamed. He cried. He prayed. He sought the cleansing which only God could give.

He pleaded: "Have mercy on me, O God, according to your unfailing love; according to your great compassion blot out my transgressions. Wash away all my iniquity and cleanse me from my sin. For I know my transgressions, and my sin is always before me. ... Create in me a pure heart, O God, and renew a steadfast spirit within me" (Psa. 52:1-3, 10). What sort of heart do you have? Don't tolerate the sinful and shameless heart which is gradually hardening to the degree that it cannot even approach God. Don't commit the "sin unto death" which would make it useless for those who love you to pray for you any longer. Develop a spiritually tender heart which fears and hates sin, one which seeks after God through obedience to his will. It is the best guarantee that your life will stay on track with your Lord.

13 / Power to Do Right

"I want to be a Christian and live my life under the Lord-ship of Jesus," he said. "But I've struggled with these things for a long time and can't beat them. There's just no point in fooling myself any longer."

"Hold on!" I said. "If you could take care of these things for yourself, you wouldn't need Jesus. You'll never know how to defeat sin in your life until you become a child of God and allow him to help you deal with your problems."

She had become a Christian two years before. Things had gone well for a time, and evidences of spiritual growth could be seen in her life. Then she got tangled up in a sinful situation. She was so ashamed of what had happened that she cut herself off from her Christian friends, stopped attending worship services, and withdrew into a shell of oppressive guilt.

What would you have told her? About God's continued love for his children? About starting over? About forgiveness? About renewed strength for the future? You would probably have spoken about all those things. But what do you tell yourself *when you are the one wrestling with failure and guilt?*

The most incredible fact of *past* human experience is the incarnation and all that followed with that event. Deity actually came to earth and lived among sinful human beings. The Eternal Word (i.e., the Logos) "became flesh and lived for a while among us" (John 1:14a). Christ Jesus "made himself nothing, taking the very nature of a servant, being made in human likeness. And being found in appearance as a man, he humbled himself and became obedient to death — even death on a cross" (Phil. 2:7-8).

The most incredible fact of *present* human experience is that Jesus lives in Christians. We have become his, and he is ours! We gave him our old, sinful, and ruined selves; he gave us new, purified, and heaven-bound lives! "I have been crucified with Christ and *I no longer live, but Christ lives in me.* The life I live in the body, I live by faith in the Son of God, who loved me and gave himself for me" (Gal. 2:20).

In this final chapter of *Young People and Their Lord,* the theme is power, assurance, and victory. You can overcome evil and live a Christ-honoring life by the power of God in you.

Have you ever read Paul's confession of weakness and struggle in his own life? "I want to do what is right," he says, "but I keep doing things that are sinful. I say I'll never be involved in a certain wrong thing again, but no sooner do I turn around than I'm doing it again. I feel terrible about myself!" (cf. Rom. 7:14-24). Sound familiar?

Paul discovered the "secret" of living a sober, righteous, and godly life. It was not in himself but in Christ. Specifically, it had to do with the spiritual strength the Son of God gives through his Spirit. "If *by the Spirit* you put to death the misdeeds of the body," he said, "you will live" (Rom. 8:13b). It is "by the Spirit" that Christian young people can conquer lust, greed, and prejudice. It is by the power of "his Spirit in your inner man" (cf. Eph. 3:16-17) that you will conquer past involvement with drugs or sins of the tongue and learn to exhibit Christ in your life.

Christians are people "in Christ." We have been baptized into him; we are members of his spiritual body. But as surely as believers are in Christ, the Bible also teaches that Christ is in believers. How can it be? Think of the air surrounding us. We are in it, and without it we could not live. Yet we live not merely because we are in the air but also because the air is in us. We take it into our lungs and sustain our very lives by its presence in us. Nothing mystical about that. We are in the air, and the air is in us. So it is with our relationship to Christ. We are in him, and he is in us.

Fathoming a "Mystery"

Do you enjoy a good mystery? Most young people can become engrossed in a tale of mystery told or acted by masters of suspense. I can recall with fondness the hours I spent as a teen-ager reading the adventures of Sherlock Holmes. My mind would race with that of the master sleuth in selecting and sorting clues until the baffling cases were solved.

There are several things in the New Testament which are called "mysteries." But do not be misled by the term. The word so translated in our English Bibles does not denote something incomprehensible and unfathomable. Instead, it refers to that which was once hidden but is now revealed.

This is the type of mystery which is contained in Scripture. Once-hidden truth becomes known through revelation. Like so many Dr. Watsons before Sherlock Holmes, we stand open-mouthed and amazed. But there are the facts being laid before us. We simply have to open our eyes to see.

The most glorious mystery in all the Bible is the one revealed in Colossians 1:24-27. "Now I rejoice in what was suffered for you, and I fill up in my flesh what is still lacking in regard to Christ's afflictions, for the sake of his body, which is the church. I have become its servant by the commission God gave me to present to you the word of God in its fullness — the *mystery* that has been kept hidden for ages and generations, but is now disclosed to the saints. To them God has chosen to make known among the Gentiles the glorious riches of *this mystery,* which is *Christ in you,* the hope of glory."

The wondrous fact of "Christ in you" is the bringing to completion of all the grand designs of God from eternity! Christ at the Father's right hand is glorious. Christ free to needy sinners is precious. But Christ in the very being of an individual is most precious of all.

A loaf of wholesome bread on the table is a welcome sight

to a starving man, but if he were unable to get it within him he would still die of starvation. A powerful antibiotic which is the specific remedy for a dying woman may be on the pharmacist's shelf, but it does her no good until it is in her. These illustrations point to the need that we have regarding Christ. It is not so important to memorize facts about him or to stand in awe of his wondrous deeds as it is crucial to be in him and to have him in us.

The first time Colossians 1:27 really burst into my consciousness was several years ago. A man whose name I cannot even recall began a short talk on this verse by teasing his audience with a "mystery." He said, "In my coat pocket, I have *something that was alive, is now dead, and which will come back to life in front of your eyes.* Think now. What could it be?"

He built up the suspense for several minutes. He had one person's attention! I wasn't about to leave without knowing what was in his pocket. Finally, after several people had guessed aloud what he was hiding, he said, "No, you'll never get it right. Let me show you. Watch closely!" And he proceeded to pull a leather glove from his pocket. "This was once alive," he said, "as a cow walking about in someone's pasture. When she was killed, part of her hide became this glove you see. It was alive, but now it is dead."

Two parts of the mystery were clear, but the third was in doubt. He didn't keep his audience waiting. He said, "But what of making this thing come to life before your eyes? This is the hard part of the mystery, so I bid you pay close attention. Are you ready? Here goes!" He held up the glove and slowly inserted his hand into it.

Why the Explanation Fits

Perhaps you are still wondering about the connection between the two "mysteries" above. The glove illustration is a simple way to explain the outstanding features of the *glorious mystery* of Colossians 1:27.

First, recall that the glove had **no life of itself.** A limp leather glove lying on a table or folded inside a coat pocket is dead. Nothing done to it by way of commanding or threatening could ever make one come to life.

All of us are in the same condition until Christ begins his work in us. We are dead through the trespasses and sins we have committed (Eph. 2:1). We are "helpless" (Rom. 5:6) to change our situation and are in the position of being "enemies" (Rom. 5:10) of God. All this is true because the wages of sin is death (Rom. 6:23) and we have all sinned (Rom. 3:23).

Spiritually dead, separated from God, under sentence of divine wrath — we have no life of ourselves. Displeased and miserable as we may be in sin, there is nothing we can do of ourselves to remove the curse. No commands, no threats, no lift-yourself-by-your-bootstraps theology can restore spiritual life to a lost soul. Self-redemption and works of merit are preposterous absurdities.

Second, remember that the glove's **new life came from an external source.** No scientific marvel or magical incantation can cause a leather glove to come to life. Its life had to come from an outside source. To be sure, even then the glove did not have an independent life. It took the characteristics of another living object by virtue of being filled with that object.

This is the sort of thing that happens in the process of salvation. The old man is dead in trespasses and sins. Yet no worldly wisdom, no philosophical system, no Christless religion can revive him. If even one sinner is brought to spiritual life, it will be because life has come to him from an external source. To say it another way, only when Christ dwells in us and animates our very beings do we have life. Without Christ you are dead. With him, you come to life. "It is no longer I who live," said Paul, "but Christ who lives in me." The apostle understood that the new life one lives in Jesus is not an independent life; it is utterly and totally dependent on Jesus.

The Bible presents the Son of God as the source of all spiritual life. The Gospel of John uses the motif of life in Jesus from beginning to end. "In him was *life,* and that life was the light of men" (1:4). "For my Father's will is that everyone who looks to the Son and believes in him shall have *eter-*

nal life" (6:40). "I have come that they may have *life* and have it to the full" (10:10). "Now this is *eternal life*: that they may know you, the only true God, and Jesus Christ, whom you have sent" (17:3). "Jesus did many other miraculous signs in the presence of his disciples which are not recorded in this book. But these are written that you may believe that Jesus is the Christ, the Son of God, and that by believing *you may have life in his name*" (20:30-31).

Jesus Christ is our life. Only as we are in him and have him dwelling in us can we share life, *spiritual* life, *eternal* life.

Third, notice that the glove **takes on the characteristics of the life inside itself.** The leather glove with a living hand inside it is no longer what it once was. It will never again be part of a grass-eating, milk-producing animal. It is now an extension of the person whose hand is inside it. Its life is no longer that of a cow but of a human being. It has no will of its own but is dependent on the will of the one who animates it.

The young man or woman who has been brought to spiritual life in Christ takes on the characteristics of the life of Jesus. No longer a pawn of Satan to serve the purposes of sin, the believer reflects the very image of the Son of Man. Just as a snug-fitting glove shows the details of the hand within it, so the Christian who cleaves to his Lord presents Christ to others through his character and words. There is no desire to go back to the old way of life, for he now belongs to the one who has given him life. He submits to the will of the Savior and has no will independent of his.

The redeemed person readily admits that he does not belong to himself but to Christ. "You are not your own; you were bought at a price. Therefore honor God with your body" (1 Cor. 6:19b-20). "Therefore, I urge you, brothers, in view of God's mercy, to offer your bodies as living sacrifices, holy and pleasing to God — which is your spiritual worship" (Rom. 12:1).

A Spiritual Life

A spiritual life is one lived under the control and in the power of the Spirit of God. [Note: The New Testament refers to the Holy Spirit as "the Spirit," "the Spirit of God," or "the Spirit of Christ." The terms are interchangeable, as Romans 8:9 demonstrates.]

First, it is a life **under the control of the Spirit.** But what does that mean? Does the Spirit of Christ in a young person pull her around, as if by bits in a horse's mouth? Of course not. The control of the Spirit is not some sort of direct intervention which cancels out a human will and causes anyone to live in a way foreign to her own desires.

The controlling influence in any person's life is that factor which is most prominent in his thoughts and actions. To speak of a seafaring man or a business woman communicates a clear thought; he is committed to the life of the sea and she has committed herself to a career in business. Why, then, should the concept of a "spiritual person" be vague? Such an individual is given over to the things of the Spirit, committed to the life of the Spirit of God, and always seeking to follow the will of Christ.

This feature of the spiritual life is best summed up in Paul's words: "Those who live in accordance with the Spirit have their minds set on what the Spirit desires" (Rom. 8:5b).

Second, a spiritual life is lived **in the power of the Holy Spirit.** It is one thing to give your life to a noble and great cause; it is something else again to find the ability to keep to that cause and reach a successful end. The Bible not only marks the right path for a human life but assures strength to those who will travel it.

The Holy Spirit convicts the world of sin through the preaching of the gospel by human ministers (John 16:8; cf. Acts 2:37). One learns of his situation before God and of his inability to save himself; he also learns of the atoning work of Christ on his behalf. As he is drawn toward the cross, the desire for salvation grows within him. But there may also be an increased awareness of sin, unworthiness, and weakness. After all, he may have struggled against sin before. He failed in his attempt to defeat evil, and he may despair of being defeated by it again after becoming a Christian.

What hope or assurance can be given such a person? The Bible tells him that children of God have special help in living their new life. Once born of the water and the Spirit, the saved person is given the "gift of the Holy Spirit" (Acts 2:38; cf. Gal. 4:6). In his new Spirit-controlled life, he will be strengthened with divine power for his struggle (cf. Eph. 3:16; 1 John 4:4). What has been lacking in past struggles with sin will be supplied now from a divine source. The power that was seen only temporarily in miraculous deeds in the first Christian century abides perpetually through the Christian Age to help the people of God live victoriously.

The teen-ager who is living a spiritual life grows in knowledge of the Spirit-given Word of God and bears the fruit of the Spirit in daily living to the glory of God. He or she draws on the divine strength which is constantly available to him and, in that power, experiences the victorious life Jesus came to make possible.

The Hard Part of Being a Christian

The *easy part* of Christianity is the taking of a free gift. That is exactly what salvation is. "The free gift of God is eternal life in Christ Jesus our Lord" (Rom. 6:23b).

The *hard part* of Christianity is the daily surrender that goes with having Christ in us. Just enough of the old tendencies to selfishness, pride, and rebellion remain to allow Satan an occasional entrance. If that entrance is not closed quickly, he can reclaim us.

As love for the Son of God grows, sin has less luster in our eyes. As we continue to focus on Christ, fewer things of this world can distract us from a close daily walk with him.

Holiness begins to be realized in your life, and your life begins to be a magnet to draw other persons to the Savior. It is not so much what you *don't do* that is identifying you with Christ but what you *are*. Worldly, immoral, and sinful living have been replaced with a Christ-honoring way of life.

At the same time, there is no holier-than-thou attitude in the person who is experiencing this spiritual walk with the Lord. There is sensitivity to people who are still outside Christ's body or who are still caught in the traps of alcohol or fornication.

In the original text of the New Testament, the same word used to describe the change in Jesus on the Mount of Transfiguration (Matt. 17:1-3) is used of the change that takes place in the lives of Christians in the course of our spiritual maturity. It is the Greek word from which we get our English "metamorphosis." Paul writes: "And we, who with unveiled faces all reflect the Lord's glory, are being transformed [i.e., are undergoing metamorphosis] into his likeness with ever-increasing glory, which comes from the Lord, who is the Spirit" (2 Cor. 3:18).

Conclusion

A real estate agent was showing a prospective buyer around an old building he was trying to unload. It had been empty for months and needed many repairs. Vandals had damaged the doors, broken many of the windows, and scattered trash around the interior. As he showed his client around, he took pains to say that he would replace the broken windows and have the garbage cleaned out.

"Forget about repairing this old place," the buyer said. "When I get title to this place, I'm going to tear it down and build something completely different. I don't want the building; I want the site."

Compared to what God has in mind for human lives, our efforts at self-improvement are as pointless as replacing window panes and taking out trash from a house slated for destruction. When anyone turns his or her life over to Jesus, the old life is finished and a new creation is begun. "Therefore, if anyone is in Christ, he is a new creation; the old has gone, the new has come!" (2 Cor. 5:17).

What Jesus wants in your life is the *site* and your *permission to begin building!*

Your life under his Lordship is the beginning of an adventure that will reach all the way to eternity.